Otto Sander in **Death Destruction and Detroit**. Schaubühne am Halleschen Ufer, Berlin, 1979

Robert Wilson

The Theater of Images

SECOND EDITION

The Contemporary Arts Center, Cincinnati
The Byrd Hoffman Foundation, New York

HARPER & ROW, PUBLISHERS, New York
Cambridge, Philadelphia, San Francisco, London
Mexico City, São Paulo, Singapore, Sydney

Designed by Michael Bierut

Library of Congress Cataloging in Publication Data
Main entry under title:

Robert Wilson, the theater of images.

1. Wilson, Robert, 1941–   .
I. Contemporary Arts Center (Cincinnati, Ohio) II. Byrd Hoffman Foundation.
PN2287.W494R6 1984   790.2′092′4
83-48839
ISBN 0-06-015289-3
      84 85 86 87 88 10 9 8 7 6 5 4 3 2 1
ISBN 0-06-091138-7 (pbk.)
      84 85 86 87 88 10 9 8 7 6 5 4 3 2 1

Contents

Acknowledgments   **8**

Robert Wilson's Stage Works: **10**
Originality and Influences
John Rockwell

Robert Wilson: **32**
from a Theater of Images
Robert Stearns

Time to Think   **54**
Calvin Tomkins

Robert Wilson: **96**
Current Projects
Laurence Shyer

Biography   **152**

Catalogue of the exhibition   **156**

8

To characterize Robert Wilson's *metier* as a summation of his activities as a teacher, writer, sculptor, painter, designer, architect and theater director would be to emphasize the diversity of his talents and overlook the coherence which underlies his work. The organization of this exhibition has been a challenging one because, even if for Wilson all these activities are one, we have had to draw upon the foundations of these many disciplines often finding ourselves in new and exciting territories.

Our purpose in presenting these works within the visual art context is not done simply to comment upon Wilson's *oeuvre* as visual art but to expand our perception as we continue to view and review the impact of many arts upon the visual world.

My foremost and deepest gratitude must go first to Bob, for his generous sharing of his resources, information and above all his trust which I have felt throughout this project. Not only has he made this exhibition possible but also immensely rewarding for me and for all of us at The Center and everyone in Cincinnati with whom he has come in contact. My respect for Bob has grown since our friendship began in 1975 when we arranged to install and produce *Spaceman* in 1976 at The Kitchen Center.

Of course, my sincerest appreciation is extended to the lenders of works to the exhibition. As collectors of these works, they not only enhance their surroundings with objects and images which are meaningful to them but also, through their support, assist Bob in continuing his work on new projects.

I am particularly grateful to Paul Walter, an avid supporter of Wilson's and a trustee of The Byrd Hoffman Foundation, who has provided much encouragement to me throughout this project.

All the staff at the Byrd Hoffman Foundation have been of immense assistance. My special thanks to Robert Liebowitz for his archival and photodocumentary assistance and to Robert Levitan and Jean Rigg for their assistance. To Lois Bianchi, however, must go my greatest thanks for her constant, efficient and diligent attention to detail which has made the project a true joy.

To Benedict Pesle of Artservice, Paris, go my warmest thanks, not only for her hospitality and assistance to me in Paris, but for her continuing support and efforts to bring the works of progressive and innovative artists to broad attention in Europe.

Throughout, Marian Goodman, of Marian Goodman Gallery/Multiples has provided invaluable assistance and constant encouragement and my gratitude for her help is extended also to her assistants Diane Harris and Mary Efron. My good friends, Paula Cooper and Douglas Baxter, of Paula Cooper Gallery have offered their resources again and I thank them for not only lending works to the exhibition but for assistance in locating many others.

Sincere thanks to the staff of the Ohio Foundation on the Arts and its Statewide Art Services program which had handled many of the shipping arrangements. Specifically, I would like to thank OFA Director Ruth K. Meyer, SAS Program Director Mary Ellen Acurio and Greg Bowersock, Jerry Pyle and Roger Dzwonczyk.

I wish to extend my sincere gratitude to Suzanne Delehanty, the entire staff and the Board of the Friends of the Roy R. Neuberger Museum at the State University of New York College at Purchase for their support and enthusiasm in participating in this exhibition.

In recognizing the staff of The Contemporary Arts Center, I thank each and every person for their ready and able assistance at every step. My thanks again to Ruth K. Meyer, whose early assistance as The Center's

Curator was invaluable; to Jean Marie Baines, Assistant to the Director; James Rosenberger, Director of Audience and Program Development; Nancy Glier, Business Manager; Pat Thomson, Director of Education; Carolyn Brown, who, as Bookstore Manager, has also assisted in the publication of this catalogue; Merle Carter, Librarian and facilitator of translations; Stephen Jenkins, Preparator and his assistant Phillip Boyd for their attention to the details and accomplishment of a superlative installation; and particularly to Sheri Lucas, Curatorial Assistant for the management of the volume of details relating to the loans, transportation and registration of the works. Several non-permanent staff members have been of invaluable service and I thank Janus Small, graduate student in the University of Cincinnati's Arts Administration program for her constant help throughout the project; Michael Bierut is to be congratulated for his design of this catalogue and the graphic treatment of all aspects of the exhibition. My special thanks also to Rebecca Merritt for preparation of the manuscript, to William Lowery, Security and to all of our volunteers and student interns.

As always, my deep appreciation and gratitude for their continuing support and trust go to the entire Board of Trustees of The Contemporary Arts Center.

This exhibition and catalogue has been made possible by a grant from the National Endowment for the Arts, a federal agency, Washington, D.C., and The Center extends its sincerest thanks as well to the Ohio Arts Council for continuing support of our programs. Support from the Cincinnati community has been vital and my gratitude is extended to all the donors of the Cincinnati Fine Arts Fund and especially to Mr. and Mrs. Robert Schneebeck for their most important contribution to this exhibition.

Finally, I want to thank John Rockwell of the *New York Times* for his essay which offers a distinctive view of Wilson's work in the tradition of the theater.

Robert Stearns
Director
Cincinnati, 1980

Heartfelt thanks and words of praise are due Robert Stearns of the Walker Art Center, Minneapolis, who originally produced this work; Ronald Vance of The Byrd Hoffman Foundation and Carolyn Krause of The Contemporary Arts Center for their aid in producing this revision; Silas Jackson of Byrd Hoffman for his excellent assistance with the collection; Calvin Tomkins and Laurence Shyer for their insightful profiles; and most especially Robert Wilson, who made himself available, throughout a horrendous working schedule, to oversee this production.

Craig Nelson
Harper & Row, Publishers
1984

10 Robert Wilson's Stage Works: Originality and Influence

John Rockwell

A first encounter with any of Robert Wilson's major stage works can be literally overwhelming. The sheer beauty of his theatrical visions, the dreamy rightness of the action, the hypnotic blend of non-linear disjunction and deeper coherence— all of these seize one's attention and, if one is particularly susceptible to Wilson's power, compel one into thinking that nothing like this can ever have happened on a stage before.

Which is correct, strictly speaking. Like all great innovators of the theater, Robert Wilson is a bona-fide original. But like most originals, he did not spring out of a void. He has always been eagerly willing to acknowledge the work of his collaborators—so much so that the credits on the program for a piece like *Einstein on the Beach* became positively Byzantine. Similarly with influences outside of his immediate circle, both from the present and the past: reminiscences of everything from earlier theatrical pioneers to painters to psychotherapy to dance to every sort of All-American pop-cultural effluvia crop up in his work. But that hardly invalidates it, nor need lessen our appreciation of his individuality. Great originals manifest such a powerful artistic personality that influences are subsumed into them. For all the crucial contributions of—in the case of *Einstein*—Andrew deGroat, Lucinda Childs, Christopher Knowles, Samuel M. Johnson and Beverly Emmons, not to speak of Philip Glass, any Wilson work remains indisputably a Wilson work.

The visual arts were dominant in the New York vanguard arts community of the 1960's, the community from which Wilson emerged. Because of that dominance, and because Wilson himself was a painter, it was only natural for early commentators to stress his kinships with the visionary, post-Surrealist and mystical-structural painters of that time. Those kinships and influences remain real ones, but the fact is that Robert Wilson is above all a man of the theater. He works in theater, he makes stage-plays (or "operas" as he insists on calling them), and his achievement can be discussed first of all in light of the principal theatrical reformers of the past century.

Overly simplified as it may seem, the theatrical innovations of the last one hundred years might best be visualized as falling into two camps: the visionary-mystical, and the naturalistic-sociological. In other words, there has been a crucial sort of drama that emerged in the 19th century as a parallel to the bourgeois novel, and evolved into progressive naturalism, Epic theater and the politically conscious agit-prop activism of more recent times. The middle-brow dramas that still clutter up Broadway, London's West End and many of the regional theaters in America today are only a watered-down anachronism left over from naturalism, and for the most part can't count as serious art.

The opposite of this movement is the visionary-mystical, which can be seen as descending from Richard Wagner (and many of the leading figures of the naturalistic-sociological school, in turn, were conscious anti-Wagnerians). And it is to this school that Robert Wilson most definitely belongs.

Wagner himself had his antecedents, to be sure—the Greeks (the source of most German Idealism), the Florentine Camerata, which invented opera in the late 16th century as an attempt to recreate the Greek drama, the reformist efforts of Gluck and the latent idealism in Beethoven's symphonic dramas. But like Wilson, Wagner was an original.

Wagner's principal theoretical contribution was the notion of the *Gesamtkunstwerk,* or total work of art. This meant different things at different times for him, as his ideas evolved and were modified by his own practice. Essentially, it means a union of the arts with the understanding that each individually lacks self-sufficiency. For Wagner, Greek drama (which, it will be recalled was chanted-sung throughout, although

the music has now been lost) was a mirror of the ideally functioning Athenian community, or *polis*. In that ideal community everyone functioned in harmony, no one was exploited, and each individual could express himself to the utmost of his ability (as a curious blend of feudal-theological imagery and visionary Socialist anticipation of Marx's classless society, this is subject to interpretations from both the political left and right, which has led to confusion about Wagner's own essentially apolitical views).

Wagner hoped with his "music-dramas", which he naturally considered a wholly different and infinitely higher artform than the mere "operas" of his day, that he could hasten the reconstruction of an ideal society by offering models of a reconstructed total work of art. In other words, the arts had fallen apart from their primordial unity, much as the collapse of the Tower of Babel had fragmented languages into myriad mutually incomprehensible dialects. Like Siegfried and his sword, Wagner proposed to reforge the arts into a whole.

Later in his life, however (the initial theory for the *Gesamtkunstwerk* was an aftermath of his hot-headed participation in the failed Revolution of 1848), Wagner slightly reconsidered the relationship of the separate arts within the music dramas. Partly under the influence of Schopenhauer, the philosopher, who valued music above the other arts, he began to assert the primacy of music, and thus by extension to suggest that the individual arts might contain within themselves the totality expressed more overtly by the *Gesamtkunstwerk*. In moving towards that position, Wagner was approaching the ideas espoused by Charles Baudelaire in his notion of the *correspondences* between the arts.

Wagner's works and ideas had a profound impact on European cultural life in the late 19th century (he died in 1883). That influence is impossible to trace here, although Elliott Zuckerman has made an

12

intriguing if not entirely satisfactory stab at it in his book, *The First Hundred Years of Wagner's Tristan.* Suffice it to say that his influence extended far beyond the world of opera and music, and that the muddled incomprehensibility and sheer complexity of his theories guaranteed what might be called creative confusion. Willing disciples, drunk on the beauty of his music dramas, happily misinterpreted, distorted and extended his ideas to suit their own purposes, and in so doing came up with original, vanguard solutions to esthetic problems that had a profound effect on the shaping of the modern sensibility.

For instance, in the realm of literature, such disparate souls as Verlaine and Shaw were both passionate Wagnerians, and used his idea of the *Gesamtkunstwerk* to write dreamy, visionary poetry on the one hand and socially conscious, talky dramas on the other. To this taste the French symbolist approach was closer to the spirit of Wagner than Shaw's. The *Revue Wagnérienne,* the leading French Wagner journal of the 1880's, was in fact a Symbolist organ. It influenced Maeterlinck and Debussy, whose dreamy *Pélléas et Mélisande* seems far more Wagnerian than anti-Wagnerian. And the review's founder was a minor symbolist novelist named Edouard Dujardin, who wrote the first stream-of-consciousness novel, *Les Lauriers Sont Coupés,* as a direct attempt to recapture the musical flow and psychological richness of the

Hanging Chair (Freud Chair) 1977.
Wire mesh. Collection: R.S.M.
Company
▶

Wagnerian music drama in prose. *Les Lauriers Sont Coupés,* in turn, was later cited by James Joyce as his primary inspiration for *Ulysses.*

These names and interrelations are hardly irrelevant to the world of theater, and give some hint of the cross-cultural stimulations that were going on in the European artistic community of late in the last century. One visionary theater person who was very much attuned to these developments was the Swiss Adolphe Appia. Appia realized that for all of Wagner's talk of a redefinition of the arts, he was very much bound by the conventions of his day, especially in the area of the visual arts. Wagner's approved décor for his first productions was typical of the heavily illustrative, detail-cluttered style common to the stage settings and realistic paintings

of the mid-19th-century Europe. In two seminal writings, *Staging Wagnerian Drama* (1891) and *Music and Production* (1895), Appia advocated a dream-like theater created with suggestions and light, a theater of intimation rather than crudely realistic appearance—in the Platonic sense, a theater of implied noumena rather than phenomena.

His ally in suggesting these reforms— and a man he did not actually meet until 1914—was the Englishman Gordon Craig. Cranky and impractical, Craig nonetheless led a fight against what he perceived to be the tyranny of unthinking realism over theatrical imagination. His fascination with theatrical machinery, robots, puppets and futuristic decor both looks backward

to the fantastical world of the Baroque theater and forward to the innovations of the Bauhaus.

Neither Appia nor Craig had much luck realizing their visions in their own lifetimes. But fittingly enough they were realized triumphantly from 1951 to 1966 by Wieland Wagner, Richard Wagner's gifted director-designer grandson, who redefined the stage-style of the Bayreuth Wagner Festival with his mysterious, hypnotic, grandly simple productions painted almost entirely with light. In fact, it is Wieland's Wagner stagings that provide the closest prior parallel to Wilson's stage settings in my own experience.

Another strong anti-realistic impulse in the theater of Western Europe came from non-Western culture. In painting and music, the impact of Asian art and Black American music was crucial. In the theater (meaning theater, opera and ballet), it was the Russians, the seeming agents of a more vital, more colorful and more passionate sensibility, who made the most profound impact. Before World War I, it was Diaghilev and the visits of his Ballets Russes that caused the biggest sensation—the music of Stravinsky, the choreography and

dancing of Nijinsky and others, and the fantastic designs of Bakst and Benois.

Because of Stanislavsky and, later, the very fact of the Revolution, vanguard Russian theatrical experimentation has largely been thought of in terms of psychologically-based theories of acting and agit-prop activism. But the work of Vsevolod Meyerhold, brutally repressed by Stalin after 1926, stands as a counterforce to these trends, and a direct example of post-Wagnerian visionary Romantics as applied to the non-musical theater.

Using the deliberately nonrealistic notions of the French symbolists as inspiration, Meyerhold developed a theater in which colors, moods, gestures and emotion were meant to blend together into one, dreamlike unity. His actors chanted their words slowly, and moved with the gravity of a church ritual. And his non-Western influences were profound: the Chinese court theater, Japanese Noh and Kabuki and Indian dance dramas.

In the 20's the German theatrical avant-gardists, although they broke sharply from naturalism, tended to advocate either epic-political theater or a mechanistic-robotic style epito-mized by Oskar Schlemmer at the

Sheryl Sutton in **Deafman Glance**,
Act 1, 1971

Deafman Glance, a play in 4 acts,
Act 1. The Stadsschouwburg,
Amsterdam, 1971

Deafman Glance, 1971

Bauhaus. In France, the Surrealists made less of a mark on international theater, but their ideas for a theater of dreams—rather like a Magritte painting transferred to the stage—not only anticipated Wilson, but the surviving Surrealists greeted his first work to be shown in Paris in the early 70's with tearful recognition—as witness Louis Aragon's "Open Letter to André Breton," published in *Les Lettres Françaises* of June 2–8, 1971, in which Aragon called Wilson "the future that we predicted."

Visionary dreams don't flourish easily in a time of war, which is why Wilson's antecedents are most commonly found in the period before World War I, in the 20's, and starting again in the 50's. The movements in present-day theater that anticipate or parallel Wilson's work are almost too numerous to mention. The disjointed mysticism of Samuel Beckett fits in here, especially in Wilson's ever-more-frequent use of dialogue. The dreamy confusions of the "happenings" of the 60's play a part, as do the more general esthetic notions of John Cage, whose determined attempts to liberate art from the bonds of tradition and stultifying form have proved so influential in all the arts. Such theater troupes as the Living Theater, the Bread and Puppet Theater and, especially, the Open Theater have had an impact both on Wilson and on the climate in which he was first received.

But there were other influences on his style that are just as tangible, even if they don't come from the directly theatrical background of most theater

Raymond Andrews in **Deafman Glance**, 1971

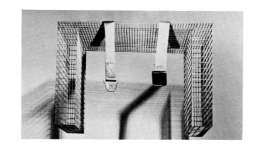

critics. The plastic arts are dealt with in another essay in this volume. But the world of experimental dance, all the way from Loie Fuller in the late 19th century, who was one of the pioneers of the dramatic use of lighting, through Isadora Duncan and Martha Graham to the sound-and-light razz-ma-tazz of Alwin Nikolais and, especially, the work of Ann Halprin and the New York dance avant-gardists of the 60's, have been undervalued in discussions of Wilson's work. The purposeful, task-oriented abstractions and childlike seriousness of Yvonne Rainer, for instance, and her remarkable blend of vivid personality and minimalist purity, clearly found an echo in Wilson.

The last influences on Wilson's style must be found in his own biography. He came to New York from Texas, which may help explain the essential Americanness of his dialogue and his quirky folk humor, as well as a curious awkwardness that seems sometimes charming, sometimes intrusive (when a stage illusion is compromised by seemingly needless clumsiness). And he brought with him a background as a painter and therapist with brain-damaged children. That therapeutic work involved games played at deliberate slow motion, in an effort to awaken the patients' sensitivity to immediate sensation. Once, for instance, he devised a slow-motion "dance" for iron lung patients, and in his early theatrical workshops he would concentrate on getting actors to execute the simplest of tasks in extreme slow motion. He once remarked that a formative influence had been a series of slow-motion films made by a psychiatrist in which the infinitesimally minute body movements of infants and their mothers were revealed to be a highly complex, highly dramatic language.

Wilson's early theatrical work grew out of the vanguard theatrical community in New York in the late 1960's. In those days the grant money

Flying Bench 1977. Wire mesh and safety belt. Courtesy: Marian Goodman Gallery
◄

Deafman Glance, 1971
▼

that is available now to New York artists through the National Endowment and the private foundations and the New York State Council on the Arts was in far shorter supply. Most artists responded by creating small-scaled, intimate works, which in retrospect seems as much a function of the socio-economic strictures placed upon them as of any innate theatrical impulse toward miniaturization.

Wilson thought not only slow, but big, from the start. He achieved his aims through the gradual formation of what can best be called a band of disciples—who came to be known as "byrds" from his Byrd Hoffman School of Byrds, which is what he called his organization and foundation. Wilson has a compelling charisma; wherever he went to do workshops or appear on panels, like as not someone would give up everything and follow him. These people weren't necessarily trained actors—quite the contrary. They were ordinary people of every

age, shape and race, from the most varied of professional backgrounds. The best and closest explanation was that Wilson functioned as a theatrical guru, and in some deep sense those who gathered around him then thought of him as a (theatrical) messiah.

My own first experience of Wilson's work came with *The Life and Times of Joseph Stalin* of 1973. Fortunately for my role here of chronicler, this amounted to a compendium of Wilson works dating back to 1969: *The King of Spain, The Life and Times of Sigmund Freud* and *Deafman Glance*. *Stalin* wasn't just a compendium. There was new material, and some of the effects were different (a Wilson favorite, a set of giant cat's legs that suddenly and silently strode in and out of the proscenium arch, was missing, for instance).

This twelve-hour spectacle was the apex of Wilson's first phase and a still-unequalled experience in my own life in the theater. The *religious* intensity of those stage-pictures will

KA MOUNTAIN AND GUARDenia TERRACE, a story about a family and some people changing, a seven day play. Presented in Shiraz, Iran, as part of the Festival of Shiraz. Persepolis, 1972

remain in my mind forever, as in the scene in which shadowy apes emerged through a forest of trees carrying apples, then watched in awe as the apples mysteriously ascended into the flies (on wires, of course, but even the visible explanation of the miracle seemed miraculous), just as an elegant human couple in 18th century formal dress emerged from the wings, the woman carrying a white parasol that was on fire.

But there were still other images going on while what I have just described was happening, and this small nexus of images was just one short moment in an evening full of thousands just as potent. And this description can't begin to convey the lyrical flow of the twelve hours, the mystical clarity with which most of the audience stayed awake and perceived the stage-wonders, and the sweet sadness when one realized that one was seeing something that could never be experienced again, by any-body. (Stefan Brecht's *The Theatre of Visions: Robert Wilson,* published in

English by the German Suhrkamp Verlag and available only in Europe, provides excellent, moment-by-moment descriptions of most of Wilson's major works, although its analytical framework is rather loose and it doesn't include the most recent major pieces).

The communal efforts that culminated in *Stalin* were impossible to sustain. After this work's four performances at the Brooklyn Academy of Music in December of 1973, Wilson could no longer function quasi-surreptitiously in the vanguard underground. Yet the communal organization of his theater up to that point, with its hundreds of people working on a volunteer basis to create complex settings and costumes, to rehearse endlessly and to allow the slow germination of new work, was impossible to maintain on a permanent basis, or to dovetail with the demands of fund-granting organizations, unions and touring

schedules. Thus Wilson's subsequent work can be looked at both in terms of his artistic evolution, and in terms of his continuous attempts—half-successful at best—to come to grips with financial reality.

The first such attempt was *A Letter for Queen Victoria,* which played on Broadway in 1974. The choice of Broadway reflected both Wilson's burning desire to avoid the stigma of the marginal eccentric, and to force his theatrical visions onto the mainstream of American culture, and his desire (naive though it may have been) to make some money from his work. In both respects—as well as his continued courting of wealthy backers—he is following in the exact footsteps of Richard Wagner.
In order to work on Broadway, both in terms of the financial commitment (he was still trying to produce himself at this point) and, it was thought, to tour, Wilson was forced to reduce the scope of his ideas. The result was intriguing but limited in relation to

Stalin. Furthermore, despite respectful but puzzled reviews from the midtown press, *Victoria* was no commercial hit.

$ Value of Man, the following year, was presented again at the Brooklyn Academy of Music. This time the experimentation consisted of thwarting Wilson's normal predilection of old-fashioned proscenium theaters (such as BAM's Opera House, where *Stalin* had played). *$ Value* was remarkably successful in translating Wilson's illusions into the close-up context of a theater-in-the-round. But it has not proved a route on which he's chosen to travel further.

The major post-*Stalin* project was *Einstein on the Beach* of 1976, seen first in Avignon in the summer followed by a fall European tour and the two culminating performances at the Metropolitan Opera in November. Organizationally, *Einstein* repre-

sented yet another approach. This time a relatively small (26, as opposed to *Stalin*'s hundreds) cast was assembled after rigorous auditions and then held together for almost a year. There were talented, original people in the cast, but the experience of such close collaboration forged them into a community almost as intense as the old byrds had been.

The other major difference between *Einstein* and Wilson's previous work was his co-equal collaboration with a composer of stature, Philip Glass. Even though he's nearly always called his works "operas", Wilson has before and since worked with lesser musicians, people content to provide original or collage snippets that can be used for atmosphere or background. Sometimes those composers have provided really effective results, as in the lovely, repetitive loop made from the "Pie Jesu" section of Fauré's *Requiem* by Igor Dejem for *Stalin*. But mostly, and especially with the recollection of *Einstein* in one's head, Wilson's music has seemed trivial.

Einstein was a collaboration from the outset, not a case in which a composer (however distinguished) supplied music for a pre-existing dramatic structure. Wilson and Glass worked out the scenario and the look of the piece together from the beginning, and both men fed off the other's ideas. The result was a landmark in 20th century music theater, the best indication of which can be obtained from the four-disc record album on the Tomato label, which has a booklet whose black-and-white photos give some hint of the appearance of this largely black-and-white production. Wilson's lyrical mysticism was lent muscle and body by Glass's structuralism, and the mystical implications of Glass's hypnotic music, always just beneath the surface, were made manifest by Wilson's theatrics. This was not an "opera" in the conventional sense of singers singing on stage: the singers stayed mostly in the pit, vocalizing numbers or solfège syllables. But in the larger, truer sense of "opera" as a mixed-media theatrical piece with prominent music, this was very much part of the tradition, and the most overt Wilson has yet become in emulating Wagner.

Unfortunately, tensions between Wilson and Glass precluded further collaborations between them for several years, or even much serious talk of revivals of *Einstein*; a revival was finally planned for the late fall of 1984 at the Brooklyn Academy of Music, which was then to tour nationally, with another collaboration on the *Arabian Nights* theme set for 1985–86. Most of those tensions came about because of the considerable losses Wilson and his foundation suffered with the *Einstein* production, which took them a couple of years to get under control. Part of the process by which he got it under control was a radical reorganization of his foundation and a decision to entrust future large-scale works to richer, more solidly established European theaters that could afford him and relieve him of the responsibility of production. Thus his major large-scale works between *Einstein* and 1984 were given abroad and weren't seen in the United States, at least in the full form in which they are only really complete. In 1979 came two major pieces: *Death Destruction and Detroit* at the Schaubühne am Halleschen Ufer in West Berlin in February of 1979, and *Edison* in Lyon, Milan and Paris in October of that same year. (*Edison*, like *Einstein*, was given a run-through with sketchy sets in New York before its full-scale European première.)

Prior to these works, however, and as a part of the process by which he attempted to extricate himself from *Einstein's* financial morass, Wilson stepped up his involvement in chamber projects. These varied considerably in scope and medium, and in every case are not only quite different but also palpably less impressive than the large-scale pieces for which he is justly best known.

That is not to say that the smaller pieces aren't important as part of his overall creative process, or that they don't fulfill important collaborative needs for him. In particular these pieces have been part of a process by which Wilson has steadily increased the amount of spoken text in his works, which used to be mostly mimetic spectacles. But it is a pity that anyone who has seen his work in America (but outside of New York) can only have seen these small studies: they just don't match the big ones.

The most widely disseminated of such small pieces, and probably the most appealing, was called *I Was Sitting On My Patio This Guy Appeared I Thought I Was Hallucinating*. This was a post-*Einstein*, 1977 collaboration with Lucinda Childs in which Wilson and Childs did the same monologue against an elegantly simple, Art-Decoish set. There have also been a series of "dialogues" with Christopher Knowles, who started as a patient during Wilson's therapeutic days and has evolved into an unusual sort of verbal, visual and theatrical artist. Other smaller-scaled projects have included a collaboration with video artist Ralph Hilton and video shorts for French and German television.

Death Destruction and Detroit was created with the ample support of Peter Stein's Schaubühne. It had a complicated set that included light imbedded in the floor—which was one of the reasons that a projected series of performances at the Metropolitan Opera in the summer of 1979 had to be abandoned.

DD&D also marked the first time Wilson had an actual, trained troupe of professional actors at his disposal, and the results were revelatory. For the first time it was possible to see how Wilson's patented scenic mysticism could work with a subtly delineated character portrayal, and how his seemingly flat and "meaningless" monologues could blossom. In particular Otto Sander, one of the principal players of the principal character (the central character usually has several facets in a Wilson play), counts as the finest actor Wilson has had the opportunity to use so far.

Prologue to Overture. Musée
Galliera, Paris, 1972

Prologue to Overture. Musée
Galliera, Paris, 1972

Preparation for **Overture**, a 24-hour
play. Opéra-Comique, Paris, 1972

Overture Chair 1974. Oak, brass,
vinyl, water, acetylene gas. Courtesy:
Marian Goodman Gallery

Cynthia Lubar and Robert Wilson in
Overture, 1972

The "central" character in *DD&D* was
Rudolf Hess, a fact kept carefully
masked in Berlin for fear of
misinterpretations intruding on a
proper appreciation of the play. This
points up two key aspects of Wilson's
dramaturgy. One is the recurrent
tendency to build his monumental
"operas" on important figures from
the past (King Philip of Spain, Freud,
Stalin, Victoria, Einstein, Hess,
Edison), and to make the "action" a
series of more or less direct reflections
on the figure, his impact and his
resonances through his time to ours.

The second is the determinedly
apolitical nature of Wilson's work, a
tendency that helps place him in the
mystical-visionary category of
modern playwright described above.
Occasionally an overt political
"message" creeps into a Wilson text,
but it almost always sounds out of
place. Even with such politically
charged figures as Stalin and Hess,
what Wilson really is concerned with
is deeper questions of authority,

terror, fear and hope, and the smaller
(deeper?) human quirks of such
seemingly overpowering figures. The
final scene of *DD&D,* for instance,
found an old woman standing outside
a wall and, in essence, lamenting her
personal loss. But she did so in a
broken recitative full of memories of
Hess's private idiosyncracies. It was
intensely moving—especially if you
knew the woman was Mrs. Hess and
the wall was a replica of Spandau
Prison where Hess is incarcerated.

Edison, naturally, was about Thomas
Alva Edison, and received its formal
premiere in France in October of 1979,
almost 100 years after Edison's
invention of the commercially feasible
electric lightbulb. Wilson has always
been a mystic of light, as his *Einstein*
had shown already. In *Edison* he
erected a moving collage of
reminiscences and speculations about
the nature of America's pragmatic
geniuses, and about American history
and mythology itself. It was scenically
less spectacular than *Stalin, Einstein*
or *DD&D*. But some of the visual
effects, particularly the dying

inventor frozen in silhouette against the fading evening sun outside his Menlo Park, New Jersey home, showed Wilson's own visual genius to be undimmed.

The period between 1979 and 1984 was a relatively barren one in terms of the public realization of major work. Several projects fell through, and much time was spent preparing the massive *CIVIL WarS* for 1984. The two medium-sized pieces that did appear had limited impact outside their cities of origin.

The Golden Windows was created for the municipal theater of Munich in 1982. A piece for a small ensemble of actors with a floating sound collage of the sort Wilson has come to rely on in lieu of a fully composed score, it placed special emphasis on its hypnotic text deployed spatially about the theater through loudspeakers. But even with a relatively modest budget, it attained

some breath-taking stage pictures. *Great Day in the Morning,* a staged concert of Negro spirituals for Wilson's close friend and collaborator, the opera soprano Jessye Norman, was given for the Paris Autumn Festival in 1982, but a combination of unrealized intentions and budgetary limitations prevented its planned recreation in Brooklyn.

The CIVIL WarS: a tree is best measured when it is down has been Wilson's major project since *Einstein,* or perhaps since *Stalin.* Originally conceived as a twelve-hour extravaganza uniting the separate but linked contributions of six nations, it was intended for the Olympic Arts Festival in Los Angeles in conjunction with the Summer Olympic Games. The idea was that, following workshops in 1982 and 1983, opera and theater companies in different cities and nations would create self-sufficient, evening-long works during the 1983–84 season, which would then come together into one massive epic at the Shrine

Auditorium in Los Angeles in June. For the gala California performances, the cast was to include Norman and another opera soprano, Hildegard Behrens, as well as the rock star David Bowie.

The piece was inspired by Matthew Brady's photographs of the American Civil War and contemporaneous photographs of Japanese samurai warriors. But as usual with Wilson's work, the "plot" ranged freely throughout man's and the cosmos's history, with—to judge from the first segment to be realized, the Dutch-French co-production in the fall of 1983—recurrent images of war veterans and miscellaneous nineteenth-century folk legends and fairytales.

As the 1983–84 season progressed, however, Wilson found himself engaged in a constant struggle to bring *the CIVIL WarS* to life in the form he had intended. Several theaters dropped out, Bowie's

The Life and Times of Joseph Stalin, Act 6. The Brooklyn Academy of Music, New York, 1973

participation seemed never to have been formally contracted, and money was difficult to raise for the travel and production costs for the Los Angeles engagement. But Wilson proved resourceful in finding substitute local sponsors, and convinced Glass to compose more of the score than he had originally intended (other composers included Nicolas Economou, a Cypriot pianist and composer, and David Byrne of the rock band Talking Heads). As of this writing, the scope of the Los Angeles performances remains in doubt, but there were hopes that a follow-up engagement of the Glass-Byrne portions could play the Metropolitan Opera in New York in July 1984.

Wilson's schedule after *the CIVIL WarS* seems full, although chat is because more and more he is basing himself in Europe, and because he is now accepting assignments to design and direct the classics as well as creating new works of his own. For

the fall of 1984, there is to be a double production at the Lyon Opera on the Medea theme—first a staging of Marc-Antoine Charpentier's long-neglected cantata of that title, and the next night a new Medea opera of Wilson's own with music by Gavin Bryars.

After that comes the long-awaited revival of *Einstein on the Beach* in Brooklyn, with the first staging of a Wilson work by someone other than Wilson set for Stuttgart in 1985— Achim Freyer's version of *Einstein*, as part of his cycle of Glass operas. Wilson and Glass will work together on their *Arabian Nights* project in 1985, with the first performance intended for 1986. In the meantime, Wilson has a new piece scheduled for the Comédie-Française in Paris for September of 1985. And further down the road is a long-projected staging of, most appropriately, Wagner's *Parsifal*, possibly for Milan's La Scala.

If the past and future course of Wilson's work seems to have been linked unduly with socio-economic factors here, that is only fitting in that it echoes the tangible links theatrical art has had with the harder realities of life over the past century. Such an analytical emphasis should hardly detract from the originality of Wilson's artistry, nor should a consideration of his influences and collaborators. The hope is that this country can find a way to support this most American of artists, such that more Americans can see his work at its grandest and most representative, and that Wilson can bring his operas to fruition in the country that gave him birth.

**Robert Wilson:
from a Theater of Images**
Robert Stearns

Robert Wilson's art is about showing us things that exist. He shows us what people do. He does not tell us why they exist. As in dreams, shapes and actions present themselves, disappear and return in other forms. We as the dreamers may be delighted, surprised or terrified, but the dream is independent and can't be controlled. Awake we analyze, interpret and try to find meaning. But Wilson's art is as elusive as the stuff of dreams. His theater is of images. He paints, constructs and architects the space of the stage and the time of our viewing with events, coincidents and objects which animate his personal and visionary landscape.

This exhibition offers objects from that landscape—tangible realities removed from the *mise-en-scène*. It might be argued that out of context they lose their purpose, become "aesthetic relics"[1] or dislocated metaphors. To think of them as such is to make them into stage properties having only nostalgic value gained through use by characters acting out a story. Rather, they are objects of specifically considered form and material, intended for real use, by real people, not playacting by performers. Richard Foreman in a review of Wilson's *The Life and Times of Sigmund Freud* pointed out "the landscape aspect of the drama, filling the stage space with real (i.e. impenetrable) objects in such a way that they are impenetrable and that very impenetrability is what satisfies as it produces awe and delight."[2]

His theater has evolved in the decade following the artists' Happenings. More structured than Happenings, his theater reveals inner worlds (his and ours) through recurring themes, motifs and forms. During the many hours of a production the stage is transformed, evolved, by objects and characters in tableaux which act upon our associations of the macabre, the naive, the brutal and the romantic.

His early works have been called a "theater of visions"[3], an "artist's theater"[4], and Wilson refers to the larger works as operas. Others have described them as metaphysical extravaganzas. At 38, he has produced ten major works of immense scale, and numerous smaller solo, duo and trio performances. He has exhibited drawings, sculpture and furniture objects in museums and galleries, produced videotapes for television and has been the focus of considerable debate among followers of the theater and the visual arts. The appearance of the work has evolved from the output of free spirited communal energy magnetized by his personal charisma to that of a lean and elegant *beau monde*. But there is zeal in his work. It is controlled, but intense. It is the zeal of one who having apprehended something of value goes out to exhibit its simplicity, not its complexity.

That thing of value is very real to him. Affected by stuttered speech, his early years were difficult. Fear prevented easy conversation. Raised in Waco, Texas, he met Byrd Hoffman when he was seventeen. Then in her seventies, Miss Hoffman was a ballet teacher and a dancer. Through her program of exercises he practiced slow and determined motions. As he learned to control external actions, he was able to relax his body and clear his internal tension. He extended this method to his pattern of speech and found his own way to overcome his impediment.

Through Byrd Hoffman, he was able to learn to speak effectively, but more important, he became aware of the potential of determined gesture and movement and how they could expose creative energy. His studies at the University of Texas, from 1959 to 1965, included theater work with children in which they were encouraged to release their own fantasies and imaginations. Later, after moving to New York City, he earned a living as a consultant for special education in New York area schools, offering programs for children with severe learning disabilities. Wilson drew from them their most constructive energies and nurtured their self-respect and creativity by isolating the child's own behavior and

Cynthia Lubar in **A Letter for**
Queen Victoria, an opera in 4 acts,
Act 1, Section 1. The ANTA Theater,
New York, 1974

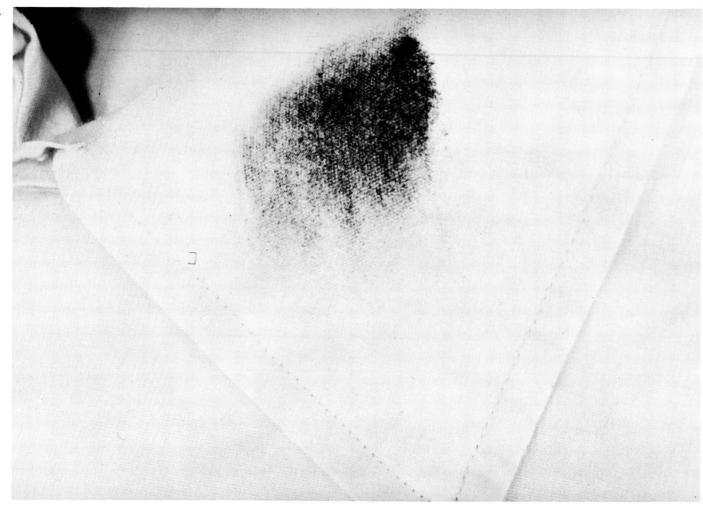

reinforcing it through slow, calculated repetition. He was able to transform habitual responses into constructive behavioral patterns by identifying the visual and spatial qualities of their actions. Most of his "clients" suffered from deficiencies of literal/sequential perception. However, they responded well to his encouragement of their intelligence for visual, aural and pattern recognition. This approach is the basis for Wilson's own work and dictated the methods of his studio and "free school" which he named the Byrd Hoffman Foundation and the Byrd Hoffman School of Byrds.

Wilson's own creative interests included painting, sculpture, theater and architecture as well as structures of dance and music. After a short time in Paris in 1962 studying painting with George McNeil, he returned to the United States to design sets for Jean-Claude van Itallie's original production of *America Hurrah*. He entered Pratt Institute in Brooklyn where he was graduated in 1965 with a degree in architecture. He spent the summer of 1966 as an apprentice to Paolo Soleri, architect of the visionary community of Acrosanti outside Phoenix, Arizona. The following summer, with a commission from Grailville, a spiritual retreat in Loveland, Ohio, he constructed *Poles,* a large outdoor environment/theater/sculpture. By this time he was already active in theater in New York City and had organized the Byrd Hoffman studio. The Byrd Hoffman Foundation continues today as Wilson's managing company, though during the years 1966 through 1976, the Foundation functioned as a

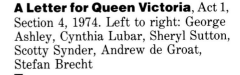

Queen Victoria Chairs 1977. Lead, brass, electric lights. Collection: M. and Mme. Michel David-Weill ◄

A Letter for Queen Victoria, Act 1, Section 4, 1974. Left to right: George Ashley, Cynthia Lubar, Sheryl Sutton, Scotty Synder, Andrew de Groat, Stefan Brecht ▼

producing company and the School of Byrds as a loosely structured workshop for dance and theater. Hundreds of people from children to older adults gained exposure to his concepts through the school. The "byrds", as the regulars are called, were devoted to Wilson. They were integral parts of his productions, members of the "family" who painted sets, choreographed the dances and wrote and composed the music. Some continue to work with him while others have developed careers of their own: Cindy Lubar, Christopher Knowles, Andrew deGroat, Ann Wilson, Alan Lloyd, Michael Galasso, Stefan Brecht and many others.

Among the leaders of the avant-garde theater of New York, including Richard Foreman, Lee Breuer, Joseph Chaikin and Richard Schechner, Wilson maintains a distinct position.

Embracing yet revolutionizing the traditions of theater, Wilson's "Theater of Visions", as defined by Stefan Brecht, is unique.[5] Although he has presented small works in some American cities, the major works on which his reputation is based have gained far greater visibility in Europe, gaining substantial production support from government and private sources.

His early works were "handmade", with the byrds participating in every facet of their production and presentation. They were shown in lofts and other locations around downtown Manhattan. The early large work, *The King of Spain* (1969) was the first to be presented on a proscenium stage at the Anderson Theater on Second Avenue. Harvey Lichtenstein,

director of the Brooklyn Academy of Music, responded to Wilson's innovations and enabled him to realize numerous works (*Freud* 1969, *Deafman Glance* 1971, *Stalin* 1973 and *$ Value of Man* 1975). Generally, however, his non-literal, metaphysical productions have remained enigmatic to the American predilection for naturalism. For the same reasons, his energetic force has been greeted enthusiastically throughout both Western and Eastern Europe as well as the Middle East. As his works are largely non-verbal, they require no translation. Through an internally defined language of visual and aural patterns, he is able to communicate equally with non-English speaking audiences and with people who do not need to communicate with language at all.

A method Wilson uses to develop a work might be compared to the process of editing film. Frames of thought, personal experiences, previous images, time, space, and color suspended in his memory provide the basic elements. Cutting and splicing, a work emerges as the collected images are collated and a structure begins to take shape through the ordering of those images. The unlikely extravagance of producing a continuous, uninterrupted presentation of all his works from the earliest experiments (1965) to the most recent would reveal the evolution of forms: vehicles, suspended figures and chairs, tall Black women, dinosaurs and animals, control rooms, jails and trials, trees, newspapers being read. He presents these as facts. Every relationship in every image is a fact. The syntax of the detail needs to be perceived if we are to comprehend one of his works—whether it is a piece of furniture or an entire opera. He gives us extended periods of time to absorb his detail and to perceive its visual and aural patterns. He offers intensely sentient experiences, and if we miss the details, we miss the point.

In this exhibition we are confronted with some of these facts and details. These drawings and objects are not remnants or relics.[6] They are more than documents and instructive orders of interest to stage managers. Drawings manifest his thinking process and provide a means of structuring his internal vision. Drawings both precede and follow the realization of a performance. Quick, small sketches fill available scrap paper as he outlines the dominant tableau formats. The drawings are idealizations which reveal the relationship of forms which will appear at the picture plane of his stage. Multiple frames form a storyboard providing a time-line sequence. They never become detaile construction specifications, yet the final sets and scrims, which are often shaded in monochromes of grey, black white, mauve and taupe, closely resemble the charcoal, ink

and graphite drawings. After a production, even when photographic documentation abounds, he continues to draw and redraw the images, reviewing his initial visualizations. It is as though the drawings are more real than the physicality of the finished work. Blocks of light and dark, volume and void are visual "libretti". Horizontal and vertical lines structure his space and diagonal masses offer counterpoint to the geometry. It is not surprising that, trained as an architect, Wilson regards the stage not only as a flat picture space, but also as a sculptural volume to be composed.

As early as his architectural sculpture, *Poles* (1967), he was interested in balancing vertical, horizontal and diagonal form. In a broad flat field he erected 576 vertical telephone poles in a square array resembling an amphitheater. Rising from a height of two-and-one-half feet to fourteen feet the incline created by the pole tops is attractive, accessible and human in scale. It offers precarious seats, an arena for some event or a jungle-gym for children at play. From a distance the simple form betrays its dimensions, yet the diagonal of the incline suggests an even greater scale as the form appears to diminish in perspective. It is stoic, Druidic and mysterious. Isolated from view except for visitors to the field, *Poles* inhabits its own landscape, a surreal image contradicting the natural site.

The diagonal recurs throughout the later works as both line and plane. As a sum of vertical and horizontal forces, it is versatile: it can suggest expanding space, velocity, a bending force in tension, recumbence, a pathway for ascending or descending or a dynamic balance or imbalance. The canted *Hanging Chair (Freud Chair)*, like others of Wilson's suspended furniture, contradicts the supporting role furniture should play. Costume drapery pulled at taut angles transforms actors into object-like forms. The angles of building roofs reiterate the closure of an envelope for the letter for Queen Victoria, contracting the scale of all

Robert Wilson in **A Letter for Queen Victoria**, Entr'acte between Acts 2 and 3

things surrounding it. In successive stages, the bed in *Einstein on the Beach* is transformed into a horizontal bar of light which alone on the stage like the hand of a clock counts the hours backwards from three to midnight and ascends silently out of sight. In *Death Destruction and Detroit,* two chairs (the *Beach Chairs*) offer tense repose for two figures who hide themselves behind newspapers which are really sun reflectors. The polished surfaces and metal headrests do not afford the comfort which the form suggests. Also in *Death Destruction and Detroit,* a facade of fascist architecture slopes away, menacing the cityscape. In *Edison,* however, a row of trees recedes pastorally behind a house.

Banal images: phone poles, chairs, drapery, roof lines, envelopes, buildings and trees. But Wilson's own intensive and prolonged gaze at these images in his mind gives substance to the forms he shows us as they reappear with altered content. As content becomes interchangeable with form, form itself gains density and becomes, as Foreman says, impenetrable.

Reinforcing our need to look and to perceive a syntax in his language of images, Wilson sometimes offers pairs of objects. They assert the importance of relationship over isolated incident. These chairs assume such personae that there is barely room for human occupants. The *Stalin Chairs,* posed at an informal angle to each other, suggest covered furniture at the summer house. Draped in lead they appear funereal. The lead reminds us that Wilson does not deal in theatrical *trompe l'oeil.* We are not being fooled by crafty imitation in sculpt-metal. This is cold, dense and poisonous lead.

The *Queen Victoria Chairs,* low seated, throne-like, resemble high backed machines of coercion. Facing off across the space, spotlights search for contrition. More than with the *Stalin Chairs,* where there is a dialogue in process, here it is a deadlock. The identical forms draw attention like a joust: comparing strength. Pairs of objects suggest the

androgynous, ambiguous, equivocal. We are drawn and repelled by the face-off. Less threatening, though no less imposing, the *Beach Chairs* are a set, not a pair. One higher than the other, a dominance is suggested. Set parallel, instead of opposing, a dependence is inferred. Highly polished metal surfaces present a tough exterior: an *American Gothic* for the brave new world.[7]

Solitary, the *Overture Chair* is removed from the world. Surrounded by a moat, its heavy oak timbers imply the power of an encastled king. A brass scepter attached topped with the flame of a jet of gas suggests not only the light but the power of sovereignty. For Wilson, the moat is but a suggestion of a vast expanse of water. He would have the chair float on an endless ocean. In another version, the chair is only a few inches high set on a large sheet of creased lead. The scale and the material more graphically emphasize its inaccessibility. The *Flying Bench* is also a machine of levitation. In the production of *Deafman Glance* (1970) a similar structure was used as an appliance to elevate Raymond Andrews, an early Wilson protégé, above the stage. Equipped with a safety belt and constructed of lightweight wire screen, like the *Freud Chair,* the *Flying Bench* contradicts the solidity and security we expect from furniture. Similarly, the *Einstein Chair,* eight feet tall and requiring assistance to mount to its four-and-a-half foot seat, was used to raise Lucinda Childs as a witness in the trial scene in *Einstein on the Beach.* Its matter-of-fact plumbing pipe construction is similar to desks and chairs which Wilson constructed as office furniture in the Foundation loft. Recent pieces, however, luxuriate in more costly materials and flaunt fashionable elegance. Like the polished aluminum of the *Beach Chairs,* the *Patio Sofa* of brushed stainless steel reflects and catches the light which plays a dominant role in *I Was Sitting On My Patio This Guy Appeared I Thought I Was Hallucinating* (1977). Used to seat,

pose and elevate Wilson and Childs, the *Patio Sofa* is an unlikely recliner for everyday use. Its backrest turns but less for comfort than to lock in or release its occupant. Reminiscent of a reductivist Rietveldt lounger its sharp rectangular planes reiterate the three window openings in the set behind. Flooding through the windows diagonal pools of light all but obliterate the sofa's hard metallic surfaces.

Wilson exploits light to mold and effect his spaces, forms and surfaces. Light bulbs, fire and sophisticated theater lighting have been used in almost all of his works. Bare, clear glass bulbs illuminate the Byrd Hoffman offices. The *Light Bulb* from *Death Destruction and Detroit* exposes his fascination with the producer of artificial light. Ironically, its filament is a helix of neon tubing.

Video both as a source of light and a recording medium has interested Wilson. Having been introduced to the potential of video imagery in *Spaceman* (1976) he began work on a series of tapes originally conceived for fifty episodes, or perhaps epigrams. *Video 50* now contains over one hundred segments which compress his accustomed time scale to thirty seconds. This series, which has no particular order or duration, exhibits his manipulation of images through reiteration, coincidence and juxtaposition. Some segments offer an element of surprise and are self-contained in their thirty second duration. Others present an image which could continue indefinitely. Superior quality technical production makes the segments of *Video 50* capable of presentation as "spots" during broadcast television

Dam Drop from **A Letter for Queen Victoria** 1974. Also used in solo performance, 1977

programming. Wilson also sees them presented in transitory locations, such as bank lobbies, airport terminals, or as installed in 1979 at the Beaubourg in Paris, along the escalators which move people up and down the outside of the building.

Wilson also exploits photography as a method to manipulate, abstract and create new images. Many of his drops and scrims have been painted from drawings which have been photographed, re-exposed and realigned. Enlarging these images for final painting by the traditional grid method has suggested an activity which he has explored intensively since 1978 during the preparations for *Death Destruction and Detroit*. Beginning with a flea-market photo of Rudolf Hess, the central character of the work, Wilson has made hundreds of enlarged details of the

$ Value of Man, a play in 9 sections.
Lepercq Space, Brooklyn Academy of
Music, New York, 1975

42

Nazi criminal as he stands in the yard of Spandau Prison listlessly raking leaves. Most of the details have become so abstract as to be vaporous compositions of grey and white. Proposed but not executed for this exhibition are outdoor billboards with several of these images, in addition to a drawing and some text material. Ostensibly advertising the exhibition, they would also extend the active space of Wilson's theater. Like the transitory experience of *Video 50*, the highway driver is given only a moment to see the image and might, but need not perceive the gestalt of different images in widely separated locations.

In the grossly enlarged details of Hess his intention is not solely composi-tional. As in all of his work, he is peering, staring into a being as if to discover and reveal its essence. But we have to remember it is not Hess, only an image of Hess, nothing more than emulsion or ink on paper. We will never learn more about Hess, nor more about Freud, Stalin, Queen Victoria, Einstein or Edison if we expect Wilson to tell us about them. But we might come to see and feel their impenetrable presence.

There is the mysterious and spiritual in Wilson's work. The theater works are spectacles, demonstrations of theatrical pyrotechnics which, if they offered a tangible message could convince and convert their viewers through their force. But his work is also aesthetic: defined and confirmed by its own form. Deeply held, even organically motivated, his expression is among the most original, yet elusive, of our time.

Notes on the Historical Surrounding[8]

The spectacle of Wilson's art uses the techniques of theater, painting, sculpture, music and movement. Its precedents are the "intermedia" and collaborative forms of the twentieth century. This history parallels discoveries made in the physical sciences and technologies which called for increasing interplay between disciplines which were reflected in the social and political spheres as well. The following notes and descriptions offer points of interests, outlining the attitudes which have motivated some of the intermedial avant-garde in Italy, Russia, France, Germany and America.

Technology and its impact on us lure Wilson as they have other innovators for the last hundred years. The avant-garde might be characterized as those creators who do not take their environment and its traditions at face value. They separate and view its elements and realign them according to their own needs. Rather than reinforcing the state of accepted affairs, the avant-garde has offered visions and revisions based on personal responses to either ethical or aesthetic criteria, and thus two divergent viewpoints have emerged. The ethical refers to the socially motivated spirit, the desire to change or affect the social order by the content of the art statement. The aesthetic contends the object asserts its own meaning and aspires to perfection through purity of form. Taken to their extremes, the ethical vision tends toward expressionist fervor whereas the aesthetic becomes a highly reduced, abstract formalism. The ethical is most often manifested in action directed toward the viewer. It is group- or other-oriented. The aesthetic is primarily passive, solitary and individualistic, producing objects of contemplation.

In the latter nineteenth century, the complacent bourgeoisie of Europe could be characterized by its taste for Neo-Baroque architecture and decoration. Its conventionalized social roles were caricatured in Alfred Jarry's absurd theater writings, especially *Ubu Roi*. In an affront to decency, Mère and Père Ubu's not-so-graciously ample genitalia were paraded before the audience. At the time the literary and theatrical worlds were the dominant *bête-noires* of society. Jarry, Baudelaire, Verlaine, Rimbaud and Balzac attacked conventional values. Theirs were ethical arguments, and their writings were tracts motivated to alternative action. Painters, since the Impressionists, have been considered to be individualistic, aesthetically motivated, and not demonstrably concerned with social issues. The Impressionists were more optically than politically motivated, but works of the Symbolist poets and painters of the turn of the century contained a shadowy, mysterious vision of the world. Leaving much to the imagination, Symbolist content nonetheless attempted to illustrate the isolation and void felt by many to be caused by the dehumanized industrial society of Western Europe.

The Italian F. T. Marinetti associated himself with the Symbolist poets, and made his contacts in Paris in the last years of the nineteenth century. Returning to Italy, he began publishing *Il Poesia* in 1905 which brought the writing of the advanced Parisian poets to the attention of the Italian community. Marinetti and his circle extended Symbolist ambiguity to the extremes of illogic in an attempt to awaken the Italian bourgeoisie. The future, not the traditions of the past, they said, was the only reality. Marinetti's *Futurist Manifesto* hit the literary and artistic community like a bombshell when he published it in *Le Figaro* in 1909. The foundation of the Futurist movement, Marinetti's manifesto attacked social and artistic convention. Futurism was an attempt to reestablish Italian dominance in the arts, and it attracted not only poets but painters and sculptors (Balla, Severini, Russolo, Boccioni and others), photographers, theater designers and architects. It espoused political involvement. Ultimately its associations with the Fascist movement discredited its achievements for many years, but its members' visionary proposals have had long-range effects.

Farrell Brickhouse in **Spaceman**, by
Robert Wilson and Ralph Hilton. The
Kitchen, New York, 1976

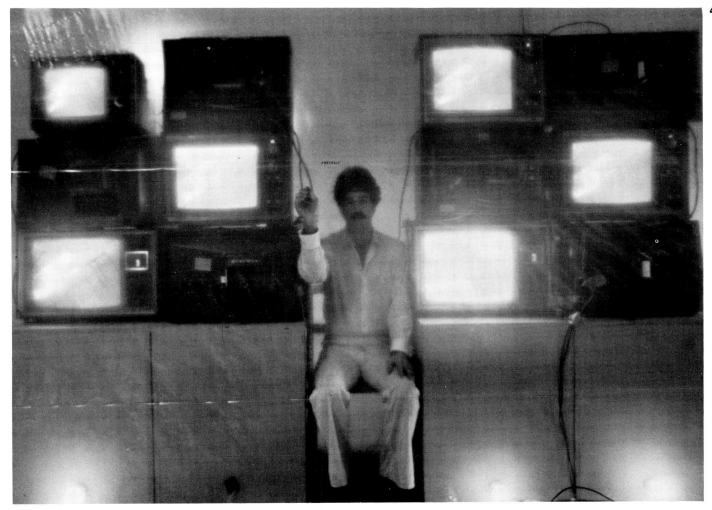

Sheryl Sutton and Lucinda Childs in
Einstein on the Beach, an opera in
4 acts, 1976.

The machine, automobile and airplane became symbols for the Futurists. Speed and the depiction of motion, "dynamism", were expressed in raucous, theatrical events as well as in the traditionally static arts. Giacomo Balla, son of a chemist and friend of fellow Futurist photographer Anton Bragaglia, extended his ideas about time and motion in painting by suggesting rapid movement through multiple images similar to the photographic studies of E. J. Marey. Later, in 1917, Balla created a staging of Igor Stravinsky's *Feu d'Artifice* for Sergei Diaghilev and the Ballets Russes. This work, only five minutes in length, called for an elaborate lighting display which, through variations coordinated with the music, visually animated the otherwise static geometric, painted forms which filled the proscenium stage. No actors or characters were ever present. Luigi Russolo, a painter by training, proposed a radical approach to the creation of music. *The Art of Noise,* his 1913 Futurist manifesto, described homemade instruments which created noises according to a chart of "families of noises." Russolo claimed that all sound—including the din of urban streets—was useable material for art and prophesized later work of John Cage. The Futurists made art which was intended to break the tyranny of traditions and allow everyone to engage in its largely momentary pleasure.

In Russia, sympathetic tremors were present. A related but independent Russian Futurist movement was led

by poet Velimir Khlebnikov and
painter David Burliuk. Industrializa-
tion had brought middle-class wealth
to Moscow and St. Petersburg, and
among travellers to Paris before 1914
a few had the means to import some of
the most important Fauvist and
Cubist paintings of Matisse, Picasso
and others. Those works were seen by
the young Russian artists including
Vladimir Tatlin, Alexander
Rodchenko, Vassily Kandinsky, and
Kasimir Malevich. Malevich and
Kandinsky held a belief in the
aesthetic and spiritual quality of pure
form. Malevich's Suprematist
philosophy was similar to the de Stijl
concepts of Mondrian and van
Doesburg. Pure form itself, he stated,
would lead by example to a pure and
ordered world. Opposed by the
concepts of Tatlin and, later,
Rodchenko, Popova, El Lissitzky and

Einstein on the Beach, Act 1,
Scene 2A, Trial, 1976
▼

Einstein Chair, 1976. Galvanized
pipe. Collection: Paul F. Walter
▶

48

others, Constructivist philosophy saw
the importance of art as ethical, as a
social utilitarian tool for improving
the world. Constructivist workers
applied their ideas to the issues of
social interaction and collaborated on
massive works for the public through
monuments and constructions,
performances and theatrical events.
Sets and costumes were designed by
Alexandra Exter and mechanistic sets
were constructed by Popova and the
brothers Georgeii and Vladimir
Stenberg. Enthusiasm was raised
through propaganda posters and
"agit-prop" boat and train
performances which travelled
through the country outside the
urban centers. Graphic and applied
design and a new architecture were
proposed for the world of
post-Revolutionary Russia.

The impressario Sergei Diaghilev,
however, had little to do with the
Revolution and removed himself from
Russia to continue to produce his
elaborate theatrical collaborations
around Europe and elsewhere.
Diaghilev was foremost a catalyst.
As a producer, he facilitated
collaborative efforts among nearly
every practitioner of the advanced
arts of the day. His sensitivity toward
the working requirements of the
artists he selected provided a creative
environment which has rarely
existed. The artists drawn to the
Ballets Russes included Balanchine,
Nijinsky, Matisse, Picasso, Satie,
Balla, Chagall and more. *Parade*
(1917), with costumes by Picasso and
music by Satie, offered an original
work of theater with machine-like
Cubist costumes and a score of music
swerving crazily between folk

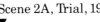

melodies, marches and raucous noise.
It remains one of the landmark works
of the Ballets Russes.

The Revolution of 1917 served to
isolate the Russian avant-garde from
the West, not only because of the
break in political ties, but also
because of the energies put out by the
Russian artists in service of the new
order. Schools and technical
workshops were opened and operated
by the artists. Rodchenko became the
director of the Museum of Artistic
Culture. His only visit to the West,
after 1917, was for the 1925 *Exposition
des Arts Décoratifs* in Paris for which
his workers' reading room *(le Club
Ouvrier)* for the Russian Pavillion
received praise from Le Corbusier,
architect of the *Pavillion de l'Esprit
Nouveau.*

Throughout Europe, the period of
1910-30 saw intensive interaction
between artists as well as social and
political reformers. A decimated
postwar Germany surrounded
architect Walter Gropius' formation of
the Bauhaus in Weimar in 1919.
Artists, artisans, poets, architects and
dramatists gathered under Gropius'
direction to create a school which was
to lead the cultural recovery. Interaction among students and faculty
encouraged interactions among their
disciplines. The stage workshop,
initiated by the expressionistic
dramatist Lothar Schreyer, was taken
over by painter and sculptor Oskar
Schlemmer in 1923, shortly before the
school's first public exhibition titled
"Art and Technology: A New Unity."
Schlemmer's innovations created an
attitude toward performance which
directly or indirectly continues to

influence nearly every visual artist working in the medium today. Schlemmer summarized his philosophy: "I struggle between two souls in my breast— one painting-oriented, or rather philosophical-artistic; the other theatrical; or to put it bluntly, an ethical soul and an aesthetic one." Schlemmer, with others at the Bauhaus, wanted to integrate the visual plane of painting and the spatial depth of the theatrical stage. Line, color, form, volume and light were used to activate the space of the stage using human figures largely as mechanical and anonymous animators of the overall visual design. "Man and Machine" had been both theme and inspiration to the

Italian Futurists and Russian Constructivists. The mechanical stylizations of the Bauhaus theater likewise abandoned traditional plots and narrative development and offered metaphysical visions of man's relationship to the world and his society.

While experiments concentrated in Europe, America was not isolated from attempts to integrate the visual and theatrical arts. Alexander Calder's work of the 1930's was progressing toward the development of his mobile constructions. Commissioned by the Wadsworth Atheneum in 1936, Calder produced a staging of Erik Satie's score "Socrates." Not to be staged again until 1977 at The Beacon Theater in New York City, Calder's work called for two vocalists who remained at the extreme edges of the stage apron

Einstein on the Beach, Act 3,
Scene 3B, Field with Spaceship, 1976

while, against a peacock blue scrim, a red disc slowly moved stage left to right, a tall white rectangle was manipulated to reveal its black back side and a hoop structure lowered and spun on its horizontal axis. Calder used the stage as a pictorial frame to display a vision of form and color in motion, a purely aesthetic and contemplative experience.

The suspension of plot and logical structure, whether in theater, poetry or painting was fertile ground for the Surrealist artist to delve into the sub-conscious responses of the audience. Release from habitual and anticipated form offer the possibility of new images with their meanings derived from the private,

Einstein on the Beach, Act 4,
Scene 3C, Spaceship, 1976

52

psychological and automatic associations of the artist and viewer. The philosophy of Surrealism is the most sympathetic to Wilson's quite independent art. It is inwardly directed, yet it maintains a contact with the world. It allows for surprises and is above all a philosophy of images.

In an open letter to André Breton, the Surrealist Louis Aragon observed of Robert Wilson's *Deafman Glance:*

> I have never seen anything so beautiful in all the world since I was born, all else pales in comparison.
>
> There are those who speak of this great Game of Silence, of this miracle of men and not of gods; this is shoddy surrealism, showcase surrealism if I ever saw it! By the time everyone is talking about surrealism one will talk of a shanty which is a little bit odd as being a Surrealist house, everyone wants (the old ones of our time and others who have come out of the compost heap which we had left behind), everyone wants to be, to call himself Surrealist and thank God! The deaf don't hear them!...Bob Wilson's spectacle which comes to us from Iowa is not at all surrealist, as some find it easy to say, but it is what the others such as ourselves, of whom surrealism was born, have dreamed would emerge after us, beyond us, and I can imagine the exaltation that you would have shown at nearly every moment of this masterpiece of surprise, where the art of man surpasses with each breath of silence the art of God.
>
> If ever the world were to change and men became like a dancer of which I spoke, free, free, free...it is by this freedom that [the world] will have changed. Freedom, a dazzling freedom of the soul and the body.[9]

1. Lorber, Richard, *Artforum,* February, 1978.

2. Foreman, Richard, *The Village Voice,* 1970.

3. Brecht, Stephan, *The Theatre of Visions: Robert Wilson,* Suhrkamp Verlag, Frankfurt, Germany, 1978.

4. Foreman, Richard, *op cit.*

5. Brecht's definition refers specifically to the works from 1969-73. Brecht *op cit,* p.9.

6. It should be noted that the sale of objects and drawings does provide important means to help support the costly productions and, as for any artist, to provide personal income. Most of the three-dimensional objects are to be produced as multiple copies with up to six "strikes" of each.

7. An oblique reference is made to Grant Wood's painting, *American Gothic,* 1930, Art Institute of Chicago (gift of the Friends of American Art).

8. These notes have been gathered from sources to which the reader is referred: Goldberg, RoseLee, *Performance, Live Art 1909 to the Present,* Abrams, Inc., New York, 1979.
   Hulton, Pontus, ed., *E.J. Marey: La Photographie du Mouvement,* Centre Georges Pompidou, Paris, 1977.
   —, *Paris-Moscou,* catalogue of the exhibition, Centre Georges Pompidou, Paris, 1979.
   Kirby, Michael, *Futurist Performance,* E.P. Dutton, Inc., New York, 1971.
   Martin, Marianne, *Futurist Art and Theory,* Clarendon Press, Oxford, 1968.

   Nakov, Andrei, *Russian Pioneers at the Origins of Non-Objective Art,* Annely Juda Fine Art, London, 1976.
   —, *2 Stenberg 4,* Galerie Chauvelin, Paris, 1975.
   Rowell, Margit, *The Planar Dimension: Europe 1912-1932,* The Solomon R. Guggenheim Foundation, New York, 1979.
   —, *Vladimir Tatlin: Form/Faktura,* October #7, MIT Press for the Institute for Architecture and Urban Studies, Cambridge, 1978.

Spencer, Charles, *The World of Serge Diaghilev,* Penguin Books, New York, 1979.

9. Translated by Susan Goforth, as quoted in Stefan Brecht, *op cit,* copyright Louis Aragon, *Les Lettres Français,* June 2–8, 1971.

Fifteen minutes before the curtain goes up at the Brooklyn Academy of Music, the cast assembles on the stage—a hundred and forty-four people, who join hands and stand quietly in a circle, feeling the energy build. On the other side of the curtain, at the front of the stage, Queen Victoria (Cynthia Lubar), wearing a diamond tiara, faces the incoming audience in a white gown with a red sash, her arm resting on a marble column at stage left. Precisely at seven-twenty, the Queen begins a strange, disjointed monologue, which Cindy Lubar seems to be enunciating in at least four different voices. ("You see, what I did was to revamp the pineal movements into wholescore glandular recollections. Arctimes besought the wholar universe perennially abiding. . . .") Tonight's is the fourth and final performance of *The Life and Times of Joseph Stalin,* Robert Wilson's twelve-hour, seven-act play, which the program calls an "opera," and which will run continuously, with six intermissions, until seven o'clock in the morning.

Cindy Lubar's speech can be heard backstage, where the cast in its circle waits quietly. The circle parts, and Wilson enters, leading a twelve-year-old boy, Christopher Knowles, by the hand. Wilson is very tall (six feet four) and a trifle awkward, as though, at the age of thirty, he had not quite grown used to his height. He has on a double-breasted gray suit, a white top hat, and white gloves, and is wearing a Stalin mustache. After studying his shoes for a few moments, he looks rapidly around the circle and speaks in a low voice. "Please be careful," he says. "I wish everybody would try tonight to be a little more reserved. Some of you have been playing to the audience, and they've been responding, but that's not really what . . ." His voice trails off. "And don't forget to listen, listen, every moment, to everything that's happening." Another pause. "O.K., let's have a good show."

The cast disperses backstage. The man and woman playing the Prince and Princess step out in front of the curtain, stand for a moment in the white spotlight, then descend into the aisle and go to their box at stage right. Wilson comes out slowly, drawing Christopher Knowles behind him. They stand in front of the curtain, neither one looking at the other, and begin a dialogue:

WILSON: Emily what?
KNOWLES: Emily likes the TV.
WILSON: Because?
KNOWLES: Because Emily watches the TV.
WILSON (*sharply*): Because?
KNOWLES: Because Emily likes the—
WILSON: *What?*
KNOWLES: The TV. Because Emily likes the TV. Because Emily watches the TV . . .

The audience's laughter is uneasy. Although the dialogue sounds as precisely timed as an ancient vaudeville routine, the boy is not an actor; he is a beautiful child with severe brain damage. He and Wilson move to stage left, toward Queen Victoria. Wilson breaks off the dialogue, turns to the audience, and declaims in a piercing voice, "Ladies and gentle . . . men! *The Life . . . and Times . . . of . . . Joseph . . . Stalin!*" At the word "Joseph," the curtain goes up.

One of Wilson's actresses once said that she liked performing in his plays because it gave her so much time to think. Wilson would like his audiences to feel the same freedom. "One of the things I never liked in the theater of the nineteen-sixties, when I first came to New York, was that there was never any time to think," he once said. "Everything was so speeded up. It was never natural, and there was no element of choice—you had to see what the playwright and the actors wanted you to see. It seemed important to me for the audience to have a more interesting experience than that." Over the last few years, Wilson has certainly provided audiences with experiences unlike any others they have had in the theater, and the reactions to his

Robert Wilson in **I Was Sitting On My Patio This Guy Appeared I Thought I Was Hallucinating**, Act 1. Cherry Lane Theater, New York, 1977

work have become fairly predictable. A sizable number of those who came to *The Life and Times of Joseph Stalin* left after the first act, offended by the apparent absence of narrative, the repetitiousness, and the slow movement, and, perhaps, by the dawning recognition that they were being invited to think—or at least to fall into a trancelike state of mind in which the imagination could run free. Others stuck it out for several hours, beguiled by the sets, the costumes, the lighting, the music, and all the extraordinary events, personages, and spectacles with which Wilson fills his stage. A third group—and in Brooklyn a surprisingly large one each night—settled without much difficulty into the dreamlike atmosphere of the work and stayed the entire twelve hours, dozing off here and there, reviving themselves with coffee and crêpes served in the lobby during intermissions, and, no doubt, going home at seven in the morning with interpretations as mixed and multifarious as the long night's activities onstage.

The Life and Times of Joseph Stalin is—or, rather, was, for it will probably never again be seen in exactly the same form—a sort of retrospective of Robert Wilson's stage work up to that point. Since then, he has gone on to do a new work called *A Letter for Queen Victoria*—a mere three-hour curtain-raiser—which had its première at the Spoleto Festival last June, subsequently toured Italy and France, and will be seen sometime this winter in New York, provided Wilson can find a theater and some backing. Although *A Letter for Queen Victoria* is considerably more verbal than Wilson's previous work, it is no more susceptible to rational interpretation. All Wilson's plays come out of his own inner imagery,

56

or that of people who are close to him, and they must be experienced rather than understood. The first four acts of *The Life and Times of Joseph Stalin* drew their basic material from Wilson's first three major productions: *The King of Spain*, which was presented at the Anderson Theater in New York for two nights in January, 1969; *The Life and Times of Sigmund Freud*, which had two runs of two performances apiece at the Brooklyn Academy later that year; and *Deafman Glance*, which was seen first at the University of Iowa in 1970, then at the Brooklyn Academy (the customary two performances) in 1971, and subsequently in France, Italy, and Holland. Much of the material in Acts VI and VII was developed originally for *KA MOUNTAIN AND GUARDenia TERRACE*, Wilson's offering at the 1972 Festival of Arts in Shiraz, Iran, where it ran continuously, to the amazement of Islam, for seven days and seven nights. All these elements were redesigned and restructured for the *Stalin* play, though, and much of the material was entirely new.

Wilson and his core group of about twenty-five close associates, who go under the name of The Byrd Hoffman School of Byrds, began to work intensively on the twelve-hour *Stalin* play about two months before the première in Brooklyn last winter. Early rehearsals took place in a loft building on Spring Street, in lower Manhattan, which serves as headquarters of The Byrd Hoffman Foundation, a nonprofit organization, and as living quarters for Wilson, the dancer-choreographer Andrew de Groat, and a fluctuating number of Byrds. Notices were placed in the *Village Voice* and elsewhere asking for volunteers. ("No Previous Theatre

Lucinda Childs in **I Was Sitting On My Patio This Guy Appeared I Thought I Was Hallucinating**, Act 2, 1977

Experience Necessary Looking for Alexander Graham Bell and Wilhelm Reich.") None of the eventual performers were professionals. They ranged in age from Duncan and Diana Curtis's seven-month-old son, Devin, to Wilson's eighty-seven-year-old grandmother, Alma Hamilton, who came all the way from Waco, Texas, to see the play and found herself cast in rather prominent roles in four of its seven acts. Among the other players were suburban housewives, students, artists, musicians, a live boa constrictor, and five children from the New York Public School for the Deaf. A columnist for the Staten Island *Register* came around one day to interview Wilson and was recruited to appear in the second act; his wife was also recruited, for a bigger role. In the first three performances, the part of Sigmund Freud was played by Michel Sondak, a designer and

wood-grainer whom Wilson happened to see passing through Grand Central Station one day in 1969. Somewhat alarmed at being told that he resembled Dr. Freud and that Wilson wanted him to act in a play called *The Life and Times of Sigmund Freud,* Mr. Sondak walked quickly away. Wilson gave chase and cornered him in a cafeteria. Again Mr. Sondak demurred, but he gave Wilson his telephone number in Far Rockaway, and Wilson went out there the following week and got him to agree. Mr. Sondak apparently enjoyed the experience, for he accepted Wilson's invitation to repeat his performance in the *Stalin* play. He was unable to come to the fourth performance, however, and his part that night was played by Jerome Robbins.

The Byrd Hoffman School is not a repertory group like the Living Theatre, whose members live a form of communal life. According to George Ashley, the *Stalin* company manager and one of the play's more active performers, it is more like an extended family. "We're very close sometimes, when a production is in the works, but then most of us want to get away and be on our own," he says. Some of the members have homes and families, and some who have been active in the past have moved on to other things. There is about the group, nevertheless, a definite sense of cohesion and shared experience. As the opening date of the *Stalin* play drew closer, the

Spring Street loft became increasingly crowded, and life there got daily more hectic. As the cast grew, rehearsals had to be moved out of the loft—first to the La Mama Third Street Workshop, in the East Village, then to Jerome Robbins's American Theatre Laboratory, on West Nineteenth Street. And, of course, there was the matter of money. The Byrd Hoffman Foundation receives grants from the National Endowment for the Arts, the New York State Council on the Arts, and other public and private donors. In the case of *Stalin*, the cost of all the scenery and most of the costumes—major items in any Wilson production—was being donated by the Gulbenkian

Foundation, in Lisbon. Under the arrangement that Wilson had with Harvey Lichtenstein, the Brooklyn Academy's director, The Byrd Hoffman Foundation was responsible for its own production costs (sets, costumes, props, and fees to professionals like Fred Kolouch, the set designer, and Laura Lowrie, the lighting director), while the Academy would assume the costs of backstage construction and of the stagehands' salaries, and contribute a modest outlay for promotion. Altogether, the total budget was about a hundred and twenty thousand dollars—a fifth of what it would cost to mount a medium-sized Broadway musical.

Wilson's main concern was that he might not get an audience. In Copenhagen, where the *Stalin* play had had its première last year, there had been one night when the actors discovered, shortly before 1 A.M., that they were playing to a totally empty house. Advance sales at the Academy were not encouraging. "Do you think it's the title?" Wilson would ask. "Are people put off by Stalin?" In interviews, he usually explained that the twelve-hour play was centered on a single incident—the death of Stalin's first wife. This, he said, had brought about a fundamental change in Stalin's career, and it also marked a fundamental change in the direction of the play; the death occurred in the fourth act—at the play's epicenter—and everything led to it or away from it. Wilson also admitted readily that he knew very little about Stalin—next to nothing, in fact. On other occasions, he would say that the play was really about our own life and times, over which historical figures such as Stalin, Freud, and Queen Victoria still exerted a powerful influence. At one point, his play had carried the alternate title *The Life and Times of Dave Clark*, mainly because the Gulbenkian Foundation had indicated that in Brazil there would be a problem about donating funds to anything with "Stalin" in the title. Dave Clark was an obscure

Canadian criminal whom Wilson had heard about. Two weeks before the opening, Wilson confided to a friend that he could just as well have based the play on Clark, and that "all those stories and associations" with Stalin probably weren't necessary. Wilson can be disconcertingly diffident about his work. A perfectionist who is constantly and intensely absorbed by the minutest details of costume and lighting and stage movement, he is bored and annoyed by people who want to know what it all means. "Why do reporters always ask such dumb-dumb questions?" he asked a reporter from the *Post*, who printed his query in her story the next day.

ACT I
THE BEACH

On a bare stage covered with fine sand to a depth of several inches, the Byrdwoman—Sheryl Sutton, wearing a long-sleeved, high-neck ankle-length black Victorian dress, and holding a stuffed raven in her right hand—sits motionless in a chair. A man in red shorts and a red undershirt is seen from time to time running across the rear of the stage against a backdrop of blue sky and clouds. The sound of gulls comes faintly from somewhere in the distance. Gradually, other figures appear. Two girls and a boy, nude to the waist and wearing baggy trousers, perform a series of slow movements. A child daubs red paint on the back of the male mover, then sits down to play in the sand (which is actually vermiculite, a powdery mixture that looks like sand but weighs much less and can be quickly rolled up in a ground cloth during the intermission). A tall man in striped pajamas (Wilson), with a stuffed bird on his left shoulder, hops backward across the stage. A soldiers' chorus advances from the wings, making a guttural roaring sound and gesticulating (five of the soldiers are deaf children). Queen Victoria comes out and makes the same gestures and sounds, which cause the soldiers to disperse and go off, saying "O.K." A giant fake turtle crawls across, taking twenty minutes to do so. A man enters carrying a live five-foot snake; he hands the snake to a follower, grasps a rope, and is pulled aloft out of sight. There is also a sort of "Greek chorus," whose heads poke up through holes in the stage apron and whose comments on the action reveal rather little, on the whole. Most of them repeat only the words "click," "collect," and "collecting," while the most prominent chorister, an Iranian girl with thick dark hair and a liquid voice, speaks entirely in Parsi. And throughout this act and the two acts that follow it a straight chair suspended from the ceiling on a wire descends by invisible degrees.

Toward the end of Act I, which lasts a little more than an hour, events reach a climax of sorts. Sigmund Freud and his daughter, Anna, walk on, following the path of the turtle. A figure identified as Heavyman, in a padded white suit, does an extraordinary whirling dance, raising clouds of golden vermiculite dust. Soon after this, the lights dim and, to the music of "The Blue Danube," sixty Southern mammies—in blackface, wearing long red skirts, gray blouses, white aprons, and pillows front and rear—do the famous Wilson mammy dance. It is hard to believe, at this particular moment in history, that anyone but Wilson would have thought of putting sixty black mammies on the stage. Even those who dislike his work, though, are inclined to concede that the mammy dance is very funny. It is also, for unfathomable reasons that go beyond the aesthetics of lighting and costuming and choreography, almost unbelievably beautiful. The scene, in fact, has led some of Wilson's more implacably vanguard critics to accuse him of becoming a mere crowd-pleaser.

When the mammies have waltzed off, the Byrdwoman is left alone onstage. She has been sitting without moving for more than an hour, now and then making a soft sound like a foghorn. The audience, watching her, grows very still. She stands up, so slowly that the movement is virtually imperceptible. She moves forward to a little square table at the front of the stage and—slowly, slowly—places on it a small green statuette that she

has been holding, unseen, in her left hand. Slowly, she raises her eyes to the audience, which has maintained total silence. The curtain comes down.

ENTR'ACTE

Following each act of *The Life and Times of Joseph Stalin,* an activity of some sort takes place on the forestage. As the audience drifts in from the first intermission, Queen Victoria—Cindy Lubar—is sitting in a carriage that moves from left to right in front of a painted backdrop of a Victorian town house, whose windows, one by one, appear to burst into flames. A man stands at the one window that does not burn, looking through a quizzing glass. While a backstage pianist plays an insipid little English music-hall ditty called "The Moth and the Flame," the Queen, who now is dressed in funereal black, gives voice to extraordinary sounds: rich, operatic contralto notes that suddenly break into shrill screams, which, in turn, become frenzied yappings suggesting a dog whose tail has been caught in a screen door. (Sitting at his vast lighting board in the wings, the head electrician murmurs, "Hit it, Cindy! I'm going to give that kid a pitch pipe for Christmas.") After an interval of silence, her strangled cries erupt into new paroxysms of shrieking. It sounds like several people, but Cindy Lubar is alone on the stage.

Again the laughter is a trifle uneasy. At times, Cindy's screaming sounds out of control. But Cindy, who had a frightening breakdown in Paris a year or so ago, is in complete command of her vocal resources. A dark-haired, round-faced girl who bears a rather striking resemblance to Queen Victoria as a young woman, she is one of the company's most arresting performers. She started coming to Wilson's classes in body movement and body awareness at the Byrd Hoffman School six years ago, when she was fifteen. Her parents were then in the process of separating. Cindy hated school, and

lived for Saturdays, when she would come in from White Plains to attend Wilson's classes. "When I was in school, I always felt I wanted to learn how to think," she has said. "I wanted to go to college and study philosophy." Instead, in her first year at a small college in Florida she dropped out to be in the Iowa production of *Deafman Glance*, and she never went back. She has found that she can do a great deal of thinking onstage when she performs in Wilson's plays, and that the images in the plays seem to relate in all sorts of ways to her own life. This is a matter of concentration, she says, not just daydreaming. Lately, she has begun to write, and some of her stream-of-consciousness texts (the "pineal movements" speech in Act I, for example) are being used in the play. Like many in the group, she has no interest in performing or writing for anyone except Robert Wilson. Cindy believes that her bizarre vocal abilities grew out of Wilson's body-movement and body-awareness classes. "I don't know anything more about it than that," she has said. "I

don't know how it came about, or what it means, or anything." The same is true of her writings, which seem to be generated more or less automatically, and which she understands no better than anyone else. She has read and reread the diaries that Queen Victoria wrote between the ages of thirteen and eighteen, but the Queen's mature character does not particularly interest her.

In a final explosion of shrieking, the Queen's carriage exits at stage right.

ACT II
THE VICTORIAN DRAWING ROOM

Some of the images that appear in Wilson's plays go far back into his childhood. The Byrdwoman, for example, has been with him for as long as he can remember. ("I just know that a very long time ago I had this image of a woman on a beach in a black Victorian dress.") The King of Spain can be dated more precisely. Wilson remembers his second-grade teacher in Waco asking the class

what each one wanted to be when grown up; there were the usual replies—nurse, fireman, housewife—until she got to Wilson, who said, "The King of Spain." The teacher noted this on his next report card, with the suggestion that this child had problems.

The drawing room of Act II (the act is based on Wilson's 1969 *The King of Spain*) was once described by Wilson as an old, musty room in which a number of odd and dissimilar characters come together without actually meeting. From time to time, pianist Alan Lloyd plays snatches of Bach, Scarlatti, Couperin, and his own compositions. Through a floor-to-ceiling gap in the rear wall of the stage we can see back to the beach landscape of Act I, where the red runner flashes by at irregular intervals. Act I was an act of passage, with figures continually moving into and out of the playing space. Act II is an act of accumulation—the characters enter and remain onstage, although they remain, for the most part, oblivious

of one another. Three gentlemen come in singly. Stalin's first wife moves about restlessly. A small boy in knee pants and suspenders stands on a low stool. A middle-aged woman in a black leotard crawls in on all fours. Another woman holds a boot and talks in Italian. A third describes the landscape in Iowa. A walrus saunters in, fanning himself with a pink fan. Wilson's grandmother comes forward and tells a story about how she was nearly burned to death at the age of five down in Mississippi; her story concluded, she raises her arms and delivers five extended, reverberant, and surprisingly melodic screams. Freud appears with Anna, and they have a meeting with Joseph Stalin (the only social event of the act). As the two men shake hands, Stalin says "Hmm." The act lasts about an hour and a half. At the end, the players move offstage in procession, leaving only Wilson's grandmother and the King of Spain, who has been sitting out of sight in a high-backed chair facing the rear of the stage. Now the King of Spain sings a little dirge and

Christopher Knowles and Robert Wilson in **DIA LOG/Curious George**, Rotterdam, 1980

rises slowly from his chair. He is grotesque, beastlike. He comes forward, raising his huge and misshapen puppet head to confront the audience just as the curtain falls.

Until the original production of *The King of Spain*, in 1969, Wilson was not really sure where he was going. Born and brought up in Waco, the son of a moderately successful lawyer, he was on the verge of graduating from the University of Texas with a degree in business administration when he decided that he wanted to study architecture instead, and came East to enter Pratt Institute, in New York. He did get his architectural degree from Pratt, in 1965, but by then he was spending most of his spare time painting. During this period, he supported himself mainly by teaching classes in body movement and body awareness, using methods he had learned some years before while working with brain-damaged children in Texas. "I

worked with a very amazing woman out there," Wilson has recalled. "It was just after I got out of high school. She was a dancer. She had worked out a series of exercises intended to activate brain cells in brain-damaged children—exercises based on the primary states of physical activity. The theory was that if we don't master these primary movements in infancy we won't be prepared for more complex movements later on. I worked with her for nine months, teaching very simple things like turning the head to the right and to the left, looking at the right hand and then the left hand, and so forth."

When Wilson came to New York, he found that his ability to work with handicapped or deprived children was much in demand. He was even invited to lecture at Harvard. He became a consultant to the New York City Board of Education and the Department of Welfare, and later was appointed a special instructor in the public schools, working with disturbed children. He also put

64

together a class in movement for neighborhood children in the Bedford-Stuyvesant section of Brooklyn, where he lived at first. After he graduated from Pratt, his activities in this field continued to expand. He worked with the aged and the terminally ill at Goldwater Memorial Hospital, on Welfare Island; with private-school children in New Jersey and with public-school children in Harlem; with suburban housewives and older people at the Summit Art Center, in New Jersey. All his work involved getting people to discover, or rediscover, their own particular "vocabulary of movement." Although he had had no formal training as either a dancer or a therapist, Wilson had an extra-ordinary capacity for establishing contact with people, for getting past their habitual defenses, and for creating a group atmosphere that was free of tensions or competitiveness.

Robyn Anderson, a young University of Connecticut graduate who was working at Goldwater Memorial Hospital when Wilson came there, and who now dances and acts in his plays (she is Anna Freud), remembers how amazed she was by Wilson's ability to get through to aged patients who had not spoken to anyone for months or years. "He could persuade them to listen to the sound of the heat in the pipes, or to watch the plants grow in the solarium," she recalls. Once, he organized a "dance" piece for iron-lung patients. He built a construction that hung from the ceiling, with dangling strings that a patient could hold in his mouth and pull, to control the lighting and the movement.

In his classes, Wilson's teaching was almost entirely intuitive and nonverbal. Robyn Anderson well remembers the first workshops she attended at the Spring Street loft: "For a while, I had no idea what he was driving at. People would come and spend half an hour or an hour just walking from one end of the loft to the other. He would tell us to walk toward a particular point in space and then to walk away, still being aware of that point. Sometimes, only one or two people would show up, sometimes as many as twenty. Once, I was the only person who came. Bob was sitting in a chair. He sat there absolutely still for twenty minutes or more. I began to feel uneasy, and even a little frightened—what sort of an ego trip was he on? But then he started slowly—very slowly—to get up, taking maybe fifteen minutes to do it. And suddenly I saw all sorts of things. It was like the complete evolution of man going on there. He was communicating *dozens* of things with his body."

Wilson's parents were not very enthusiastic about the way his career was developing. His father, who had always wanted him to be a lawyer, was somewhat impressed when, in 1961, an art gallery in Dallas gave Wilson a show, and sold every picture, but by this time Wilson had virtually abandoned painting for theater. "The real reason I stopped painting was that the images in my head were so much richer than what I could get on the canvas," he said once. Theater was by no means a new interest for Wilson, although, being a nonreader, he had little or no knowledge of theater history. (The one book he cites as having had an important effect on his thinking is John Cage's *Silence.*) Starting when he was twelve, he had written and put on dozens of plays in the family's garage in Waco; he had run a children's-theater workshop sponsored by the University of Texas; he had designed the sets and costumes for several Off Off Broadway plays, including the giant puppets for the original production of Jean-Claude van Itallie's *America Hurrah.* Wilson's early theater pieces in New York were all based on nonverbal, bodily communication in some form, and thus came closer to avant-garde dance than to most forms of theater. He put on a number of somewhat minimal works, and then, in 1968, at the loft on Spring Street, *Byrdwoman,* in which a number of people bounced on boards, leaned against wires, and

Death Destruction and Detroit,
Prologue. Schaubühne am Halleschen
Ufer, Berlin, 1979

65

otherwise disported themselves in an environment resembling a chicken coop. This was followed by *Alley Cats*, which featured Wilson, the dancer Meredith Monk, and forty other performers in long fur coats, and which was presented at the Loeb Student Center at N.Y.U. Some of the visual elements of these apprentice works, such as people in long fur coats and people leaning against wires, have continued to turn up in his subsequent works.

About this time, Wilson also made contact with Jerome Robbins. Robbins had recently established his American Theatre Laboratory, an experimental project, financed by a grant from the National Endowment for the Arts, to explore new ideas and directions in the theater. He invited Wilson to join the group as a designer, and then, after finding out about his work with children, asked him to lead a class at the lab in body movement. Robbins later helped with the expenses of *Alley Cats*, and has remained, ever since, one of Wilson's closest friends and most enthusiastic

supporters. When Wilson first came to Robbins's lab, the group there was working with elements of Japanese Noh drama. The exaggerated slow movement that later characterized Robbins's ballet *Watermill* has sometimes been attributed to the influence of Wilson, but what seems more likely is that the two men were approaching, from different directions, similar theatrical ideas.

In the late sixties, Wilson's ideas became more ambitious. Having spent the summer of 1966 working with the architect Paolo Soleri in Arizona, he felt the urge to build something outdoors—something big. Through a former classmate at Pratt, he got a commission from the Grailville School, in Loveland, Ohio, to build a twelve-hundred-dollar "environment-theater-sculpture" of telephone poles. He used five hundred and seventy-six poles in all, of various lengths, and sank them in a wheat field, so that the square "sculpture" started at two and a half feet and rose to fourteen and a half feet. The wheat farmers

Death Destruction and Detroit,
Scene 2, 1979

were puzzled, but the structure, called *Poles,* has since been used as a site for weddings and other festive gatherings, and, Wilson says, "it will probably be there for a long time."

Wilson had also been thinking that it might be nice to put together a large-scale theater piece, using as performers some of the people from his various body-movement classes. He had no difficulty finding volunteers of all ages for what became *The King of Spain.* The real problem was finding money and a theater. He had financed *Byrdwoman* mainly by writing checks on nonexistent bank balances; the checks bounced, but by then he had what he needed and could pay the money back out of ticket sales. *The King of Spain* was too big for such guerrilla tactics. He needed a large theater for the set he had in mind. Near the end of the play, moreover, Wilson wanted a cat to walk across the front of the stage—a cat so immense that only its legs would be visible. Jerome Robbins, who was helping to finance the production, was dubious about the cat legs. They would require a specially constructed track above the stage, and a system of pulleys, and at least eight people backstage to work the apparatus; the whole thing would be hugely expensive. "About two weeks later," Robbins recalls, "I asked Bob how the big cat was coming. He said, 'I've got the fur.' He'd gone out and bought forty yards of imitation fur, with the idea that you had to start somewhere. One of the inspiring things about Bob is his complete trust in his own images. The cat legs were built."

For four hundred dollars (which represented every cent he had), Wilson was able to rent, for two nights, the Anderson Theatre—big, old, and musty; just right for the atmosphere Wilson had in mind—on Second Avenue at Fourth Street, and the cat legs were installed, after a couple of near-accidents. However, the cat-leg assembly fell to pieces in Paris during the Byrds' last European tour, and it was not used in *The Life and Times of Joseph Stalin.* It would have cost too much

to rebuild. Everyone regretted the loss, especially George Ashley. "That was such a fine effect," he said sadly. "The gigantic cat walking through the drawing room, and nobody paying any attention."

ENTR'ACTE

A cowboy climbs out of one of the holes in the stage apron carrying a guitar. He sits with his legs in the hole, strums, and sings "I'm Thinking Tonight of My Blue Eyes." Wilson appears at stage right and echoes him with loud squawking sounds. They are old buddies, these two, classmates at Pratt. Duncan Curtis, the cowboy, whose father is the head of George School, in Newtown, Pennsylvania, lives now, with his wife and baby, in British Columbia in a cabin he built himself on some wilderness land that the Byrd Hoffman Foundation acquired two and a half years ago. Wilson and some of the others spend time up there in the summers, working on new material, building things, reading, writing, cooking, and meditating, but Duncan and Diana Curtis live there the year round. They like the isolation. The place is fifty miles from the nearest town.

Wilson's original idea for this entr'acte was to have another friend, Dan Stern, stand in one of the holes and talk to the audience about his work with very young children. Dr. Stern, whom Wilson met through Jerome Robbins, is an experimental psychiatrist at the New York State Psychiatric Institute, and his work has had a profound effect on Wilson's thinking. Dr. Stern's films of babies and their mothers, shown in extreme slow motion, disclose a world of gestural communication that is not visible otherwise. To take an example that Wilson refers to again and again: A baby cries, and the mother reaches to pick it up; what we see with our eyes is the large movement, the tender gesture—but when the film is shown in slow or stop motion, frame by frame, we can see that the mother's initial reaction, in almost

68

every case, is to make a *lunge* toward the child, and that the child's reaction is to recoil, in what looks very much like terror. "So many different *things* are going on," Wilson says. "And the baby is picking them up. I'd like to deal with some of these things in the theater, if that's possible. I guess what I'm really interested in is communication." Dr. Stern wanted to accept Wilson's invitation to be in the play (his name is even listed in the program), but he could not spare the time. He is extremely interested in Wilson's work. "Mothers and children play all sorts of exaggerated verbal-visual games," he said recently. "It's like a sort of dance that precedes speech, with specific action and reaction going on all the time. In some ways, it's remarkably like what Bob is doing in the theater—the way he works with people. In fact, when I see what he's doing, sometimes I wonder why I'm doing what I do."

ACT III
THE CAVE

Those in the audience who have seen *The Life and Times of Sigmund Freud* tell their friends to be sure and stay for Act III—the animal act. The setting is a dark, shadowy cave. An old woman (Wilson's grand-mother) in a tattered, multicolored garment lights an oil lamp, and in the flickering light we begin to make out familiar shapes. The King of Spain sits on a pile of straw, with the Byrdwoman at his side. Near them lies a great ox. Gradually, other animals appear from the shadows and lie down in the straw: lion, black bear, ape, turtle, polar bear, walrus, fox, ostrich. The costumes have all been made by various Byrds; the movements are wonderfully feral. Alan Lloyd's score, which he plays on a piano in the wings, is quiet, repetitive, ritualistic. The old woman sits on a stool near the cave mouth. In the bright daylight outside the cave, young men and women, nude to the waist, crawl back and forth with animal grace, slowly stretching their muscles and nuzzling one another. A heavy vertical bar falls suddenly into place at one side of the cave mouth. After a time, those outside the cave begin to stand erect—awkwardly at first, and then more naturally. Another heavy bar falls into place. The animals inside the cave quietly shift their positions. The small boy in knee pants and suspenders enters the cave, lies down, and goes to sleep.

Outside, the now fully erect creatures move about more quickly; soon they will start to run back and forth across the entrance, uttering shrill cries. Black-clad people from another time move past the cave mouth in a slow procession—priest, aristocrat, *grande dame*, executioner—the costumes stiff and elaborate, some with long trains dragging behind. Three ladies in white dance. The procession continues. Every few minutes, another bar hurtles down in front of the entrance, separating the cave's inhabitants from those outside. At the end, the entrance is closed; the cave is a cage. The men and women in the daylight slowly gather around the cave mouth, put on masks, and look through the bars; it is a scene out of Goya. And now Sigmund Freud comes out of the shadows, walks slowly to the center of the cave, and sits in the chair that since the beginning of the play has been descending imperceptibly on a wire from the flies, and has just at this moment touched the floor. Nothing moves for several minutes. The boy in knee pants begins to cry. On his thirteenth cry, Anna Freud runs in behind Freud and makes a dramatic gesture above his head, and as she does so a pane of glass falls and shatters on the stage. Curtain.

Interpretations come almost too readily. Primitive innocence and decadent civilization. Man cut off from his animal nature (while Freud looks on). Plato's cave and the shadows of images. When *The Life and Times of Sigmund Freud* was presented at the Brooklyn Academy in 1969, Richard Foreman, an avant-garde dramaturge of Wilson's generation, described this act in the *Village Voice* (the first serious critical piece on Wilson's work, and a

Death Destruction and Detroit,
Scene 2, 1979

perceptive one) as a "20th-century
Nativity scene," and called the play
"one of the major stage works of the
decade." Tonight, the spectators
respond to it enthusiastically. There
is a crescendo of applause, laced with
loud "Bravo"s. There is also a rush
for the Lepercq Space, on the second
floor, where dinner is being served. It
is after ten-thirty, and the fourth act,
as many in the audience are aware,
will run more than two hours.

In his dressing room backstage,
which he shares with Andy de Groat,
the dancer-choreographer, Wilson is
uncertain about tonight's
performance. It seems to him to be
going almost too smoothly; there are
not enough "scratches," as he calls
them—flaws and snags that require
adjusted reactions on the part of the
performers. Also, he is annoyed with
Richie Gallo, who has managed to
make at least one appearance in
every act, although Wilson has told
him he can appear only three times
all evening. Richie Gallo is another
former classmate of Wilson's at

Pratt. Now he lives with his mother
in Brooklyn and practices his
probably unique form of "corporeal
art," which mostly involves making
unscheduled appearances in public
places, such as the expensive-dress
department at Bendel's, masked and
wearing one of his skin-tight
black-leather-and-chains outfits, and
just standing there for a while, as the
customers slink away. He has a great
wardrobe—white outfits and green
ones, a wide-mesh black fishnet, a
flaming-red job with yards and yards
of trailing red chiffon. In the past,
Wilson has tried to keep him out of
his productions, but this seems to be
impossible. Clive Barnes, in his
generally admiring *Times* review of
Stalin, wrote that the play had some
elements of camp, which bothered
Wilson no end; Wilson doesn't think
his work is camp, and he suspects
that Barnes was referring to Richie
Gallo. Tonight, when Gallo made an
unscheduled entrance in the second
act wearing the black fishnet, Wilson

stood in the wings and practically shouted, "Richie, damn you, get off!"

Francine Felgeirolles, on the other hand, is behaving fairly well tonight. Francine, the French girl who plays Stalin's first wife, hammed outrageously in the earlier performances, playing broadly to the audience, drawing laughs, and rather successfully dispelling the atmosphere that the other actors were trying to create. Wilson has hesitated to speak to her about it, because Francine is so unstable. She has a history of mental illness—in fact, Francine was a patient in a mental hospital when she attended her first Wilson workshop, in Paris, in 1972. Her response to the workshop was so remarkable that Wilson asked her to perform with the group at the Opéra-Comique, which

she did, much to the amazement of her doctors. At Wilson's invitation, she came to New York to be in the *Stalin* play. There were one or two unnerving scenes after her arrival, and once she was on the verge of returning to Paris, but a day later she appeared at the Spring Street loft and announced that she was no longer schizophrenic. Wilson doesn't want to do anything to undermine her fragile self-confidence.

"I don't know," Wilson said after the second-night performance. "Sometimes I think it's O.K. what she does onstage. It's such a contradiction of my work, but maybe it's good to contradict yourself. Also, in her particular situation this is such a big thing for her. If she can get through these four performances, maybe that's more important than

Death Destruction and Detroit,
Scene 7, 1979

anything else.'' But he did speak to her before this night's performance. ''I screwed up all my courage and told her she was doing too much—that she should be more restrained,'' he said afterward. ''She seemed to accept it. She really is a remarkable performer.''

Robyn Anderson and others are often surprised by Wilson's odd mixture of diffidence and authority, gentleness and power. ''There's something almost Svengali-like in the way he draws from people all sorts of things they never knew were there,'' Robyn said one day. ''He makes impossible demands on everyone, and yet the atmosphere he creates is one of great freedom. Of course, by the time we get to the actual performance stage everyone is a little crazy and freaked out from sheer exhaustion.''

ENTR'ACTE

This is the opening scene—the murder scene—of *Deafman Glance*, and it is a good deal more than an entr'acte. It has sometimes lasted as long as an hour, depending on how Sheryl Sutton plays it. Sheryl, the Byrdwoman—still in her long black Victorian dress—starts the scene standing with her back to the audience, facing a painted drop that suggests a massive stone wall. Behind her, on a raised platform built out over the stage apron, a young black boy sits on a stool, reading, while his younger sister sleeps. Both the children wear white nightgowns. At Sheryl's right is a small table on which are placed a half-filled bottle of milk, a glass, a pair of black gloves, and a knife. Sheryl stands absolutely

immobile, waiting, until the intermission audience is seated and silent.

Sheryl Sutton's theatrical presence is phenomenal. No one else in the group, except perhaps Wilson, has it to such an intense degree. This arrestingly beautiful black girl—born in New Orleans, raised in Chicago, an undergraduate at the University of Iowa when Wilson found her there in 1970—can hold an audience in complete silence without appearing to do anything whatever. "I do so little," she marveled one evening, backstage. "The Byrdwoman is not really a character, and I don't try to make her one. Maybe it's the absence of details that makes her so mysterious." Sheryl has played only one other important role in her brief theatrical career—Medea, in a student production at the University

of Iowa. For Sheryl, the murder has three parts, each with its own particular tempo: drawing on the gloves (medium slow), pouring the milk and giving it to the children (quick), and the killings themselves (very slow). The tempo with which she turns away from the backdrop and puts on the long black gloves determines the tempos of the two other parts, and no two performances are ever quite the same. In the *Stalin* play, the murder scene took about twenty minutes the first night, fifteen the last. It is a ritual—a slow and undeviating series of movements that Sheryl has come to think of as a kind of dance. She draws on the gloves. She pours the milk and carries it to the reading boy, who drinks; she returns the glass to the table and takes up the knife; she crosses again to the boy, and slowly

Beach Chairs 1979. Aluminum. Collection: Schaubühne am Halleschen Ufer ◀

—her absolute concentration making of the act one clear line—slides the blade into his body and gently cradles him as he falls forward to the floor. The same sequence is repeated with the girl. Then, as Sheryl wipes the knife for the second time and returns it to the table, the boy in knee pants and suspenders comes on from stage left and cries out. He cries again and again, perhaps forty times, while Sheryl walks slowly to where he is standing. She covers his eyes with her black-gloved hand. Her hand moves downward to his mouth, and the cry is cut off.

Sheryl herself has no clear idea what the murders signify, or why their effect is so stunning. "Maybe that's why I'm still here," she has said. "I'm still trying to find out what it is that Bob does."

ACT IV
THE FOREST

Deafman Glance is Wilson's most widely acclaimed theater work. In its three-and-a-half-hour version of 1971, it was the sensation of the World Theatre Festival in Nancy, France; subsequently it played in Amsterdam and Rome, where it was enthusiastically received, and in Paris, where the majority of its forty performances were sold out well in advance. Eugene Ionesco announced that Robert Wilson "has gone farther than Beckett," and *Le Monde*'s theater critic wrote that *Le Regard du Sourd* was "clearly a revolution of the plastic arts that one sees only once or twice in a generation." The Byrd Hoffman Foundation could no doubt mount an extended and successful production of this play

Edison, Isabel Eberstadt in Act 1.
Théâtre National Populaire, Lyon,
France, 1979. The house with film
projection

alone, but Wilson, of course, has no
intention of doing that.

For the *Stalin* play, the *Deafman*
material has been pared down to a
little more than two hours. Several of
the characters have become Stalin
figures, and the two women at a
banquet table downstage right are
now Stalin's first and second wives;
because of this, they cannot appear
simultaneously. Both wives die
violently onstage. Wife No. 2 (Scotty
Snyder) shoots herself toward the
end of the act. The death of Wife No.
1 (Francine Felgeirolles) takes place
at the exact midpoint of the entire
play's action; she leaves the banquet
table and wanders downstage to the
murder platform (from which the
bodies of the slain black children
have been removed), there to perish
in slow agony—it has been said that
she was poisoned on Stalin's orders—
while two Stalin figures in white
uniforms (Wilson and Cindy Lubar)
sit stolidly in white armchairs and
watch. Wilson-Stalin then sings a love
song—Al Jolson style, with maximum
bathos—over her bier. According to
Wilson-author, this scene is the key
to the play—the single event that
irrevocably altered Stalin's life ("He's
supposed to have said he loved her"),
and changed the course of history.
Here it serves as a turning point in
the twelve-hour cycle.

Wilson's multilayered, architectural
stagecraft approaches its richest and
most complex effects in Act IV.
Nearly a hundred characters move
through a stage space that seems to
stretch back almost to infinity,
through seven successive horizontal
playing zones ("tracks," Wilson calls
them), in each of which various

Edison, Act 3, 1979

activities take place singly or simultaneously. The activity in one zone is continually juxtaposed with the activities in other zones, and the eye must move constantly to take it all in. Wilson has cheerfully dug down into the centuries-old bag of theatrical tricks and come up with whatever he needed—scrims, flats, all kinds of special lighting, traps in the floor, backdrops that rise and backdrops that descend, a wooden house that catches fire and sinks to ashes, even a palm tree that grows several feet as the act progresses. From time to time, this tremendous visual collage suggests a painting—a Magritte, perhaps, or one of the dreams of the Douanier Rousseau— but a painting that changes as we look at it.

The act begins with a gathering of women in long white gowns (each one carrying on her arm a white bird) sitting in white chairs in the forest and listening to a white-clad mammy play the "Moonlight" Sonata on a piano. As it gradually progresses, more and more elements are added. A giant green frog (Duncan Curtis) squats at the head of the banquet table downstage right, drinking Martinis served him by a red-headed waiter and occasionally scribbling notes to his dinner guests, who include a Stalin with one hugely enlarged eye (George Ashley) and, in turn, Stalin's two wives. At stage left, semi-nude people build a wooden bin on the backs of four large turtles. Fish people move slowly across the stage with a finlike motion. A goat-woman appears at the window of the little house, speaking in a strange tongue. Behind the house, figures move through the trees—an old man following an ox, a green-headed dwarf, a woman carrying a child (seven-month-old Devin Curtis, who evidently never cries), men and women holding large squares of glass that catch and reflect the stage lights, a violinist, Ivan the Terrible, the King of Spain. Behind them all, the red runner crosses and recrosses and behind him a pyramid is rising; near the end of the act a luminous eye will appear at its apex. The moon rises, moves across the sky, and sets. Characters speak, sometimes intelligibly. Music is heard—Beethoven, Buxtehude, original compositions by several Byrd composers. The Pope appears, and inexplicably falls dead. The dinner guests having departed or died, the frog, who has not moved from his crouched position for almost two hours, makes a prodigious leap onto the banquet table, landing on a concealed trampoline-like mechanism that catapults him ten feet across the stage; three more leaps effect his exit. A beautiful young couple dance, nude, to the music of Fauré's *Requiem*; they lead a procession of women in white into the forest and down into the earth, descending through trapdoors. Smoke or fog drifts through the forest, and a tribe of black apes moves out from the trees. Marie Antoinette and George Washington enter, resplendent in eighteenth-century court costumes, their hands and faces painted silver; Marie Antoinette's parasol is aflame. And watching it all from a bench on the stage—a bench that slowly rises on invisible wires after the death of Stalin's first wife, so that for the second hour he is looking down from the height of the treetops—is the boy in knee pants and suspenders, the boy who saw the Byrdwoman murder her children, the boy who has appeared in all the preceding acts. The boy played originally by Raymond Andrews.

Wilson met Raymond Andrews by chance one evening in 1968, when he was arriving to teach at the Summit Art Center. Raymond had just thrown a rock through a church window, and, as Wilson later discovered, he had been in trouble with the police on several other recent occasions. He was eleven then, a deaf-mute black boy from Alabama who had come North a few months before to live with a foster family in Summit. He had never attended school. Using signals and gestures, Wilson induced the boy to come to the class at the Summit Art Center. Raymond was pretty disruptive at first, but he came to the class every week from then on, and soon Wilson began taking him to his other classes as well. Raymond was wonderful with younger children, encouraging them to get rid of their self-consciousness and to move around more freely. He was also highly intelligent, and he had a visual memory that enabled him to imitate any step or movement after seeing it once—later, in their rehearsals, Raymond was often more acute than Wilson at correcting tiny details of movement or design. His deafness was no problem after a while. Performing as the lead mammy in *The Life and Times of Sigmund Freud*, Raymond would stop his movement the instant the piano stopped playing—he could feel the vibrations through the floor. Wilson also got him started painting and drawing, and the results were wildly imaginative. "A lot of the material in *Deafman* came from Raymond," Wilson has said. "Raymond was the deaf man. The play was really based on a series of images around Raymond, on Raymond's drawings, and on my thinking about him." The boy's foster parents gave their permission for Raymond to go out to the University of Iowa with Wilson in 1970, when Wilson was invited to give a workshop there at the Center for New Performing Arts. The workshop sessions became rehearsals for the first version of *Deafman Glance*, during which Raymond was never offstage.

A number of people in the present group joined it originally at the University of Iowa. Sheryl Sutton and Mel Andringa, the stage manager of *Stalin*, were both students there, as was Bobbi Krasner (Marie Antoinette). Sue Sheehy was

working as a cook-cashier at Henry's Beef-n-Burger, near the campus. Wilson and John d'Arcangelo, the stage manager of *Deafman,* came into the diner and asked if she would like to be in a play, and after thinking about it overnight she agreed. They gave two performances of *Deafman* at the university, and filmed a third. Several Iowa students came East the next year to be in the Brooklyn Academy production, and then went on the European tour that spring. So did Raymond Andrews. George Ashley and another member of the group took turns tutoring him in his schoolwork. (He was attending school regularly by this time.) He learned how to ride the Métro, and traveled all around Paris by himself, having a fine time. Toward the latter part of June, though, Raymond wanted to go home; Wilson had promised to send him to camp that summer, and the camp session had already started.

"At first, I said he couldn't leave—that he was the star of the show and we needed him," Wilson recalls. "Then I said O.K., but that it was his responsibility to find and train his own replacement. The play was up to ten hours by then, with the addition of the *Freud* material, so there was a lot to teach. Raymond suggested a young Nigerian girl who was in the cast, and I realized that she would be very good for the part. So Raymond taught it to her. And the night she went on, he did a very beautiful thing. He dressed in the white costume of the Prince—he had always wanted to see the play from out front, and the Prince and Princess sit in a box the whole time.

Edison, Philippe Chemin in
Epilogue. Lyon, France, 1979

Then, at the beginning of the fourth
act, when the Nigerian girl was
sitting on a bench on the stage,
Raymond left the box, went
backstage, changed his clothes, and
came out onstage bringing her the
black hat that she was supposed to
wear but had forgotten. He gave her
the hat, bowed to her, bowed to the
audience, danced around her, and left
the stage."

In the *Stalin* play, Raymond's role
was played by Julia Busto, a slim
young Argentine girl whom Wilson
considers one of the most gifted
members of the group.

ENTR'ACTE
After Act IV, the audience thins out.
It is close to two o'clock in the
morning, and most of those who do

not plan to stay through to the end
have gone home. The remainder—
some four hundred souls on this
frozen winter night—have a sense of
solidarity verging on camaraderie.
Neighbors nod to one another as they
come back after the intermission.
They stretch their legs over the
empty seats in front. On the platform
over the stage apron, a *tableau
vivant* has Helen Keller, Anne
Sullivan, and Alexander Graham Bell
holding hands, oblivious of a ringing
telephone. They are engaged in
wireless communication.

In a dressing room backstage, Scotty
Snyder and Mary Peer are drinking
coffee and eating homemade cake.
Mrs. Snyder lives with her husband, a
retired Air Force colonel, in Summit,
and until a mutual friend brought
Robert Wilson to a party at their

The video adaptation of **Deafman Glance**, produced by The Byrd Hoffman Foundation, 1981. Storyboard illustrations by Thomas Woodruff; performance by Sheryl Sutton

house one afternoon in 1968 she used to spend most of her free time painting and making sculpture; her work has been exhibited at the Newark Museum and elsewhere. At the party, she happened to mention that the Summit Art Center needed somebody to teach a children's art class on Saturdays. Wilson proposed himself, Mrs. Snyder arranged it, and the children's class (which turned out to be a class in body movement) soon expanded to include adults. Mrs. Snyder, Mrs. Peer, and quite a few others from Summit have been performing in Wilson's plays ever since. Mrs. Snyder plays Stalin's second wife, among other parts. A calm, monumental woman who speaks in the flat and unhurried accents of the Midwest (she was born in Iowa), she leads two very distinct lives. "My husband says I was an artist before I joined the circus," she observes. "He comes to the plays and to the parties in the loft, but he's not a Byrd. He tends to be a little resentful when I come home from a tour exhausted or sick. He's concerned, but he's a little resentful, too."

Part A, Section 12
(34 seconds)

Cut to over S. shoulder.
S. walks toward boy on stool.
(room is painted pale pastel
color, grey wooden floor)

As S. comes closer, Boy looks
up from magazine.

S. holds glass toward Boy.

Part A, Section 25
(34 seconds)

Cut to over S.'s shoulder.
Camera follows as she walks
toward Boy.

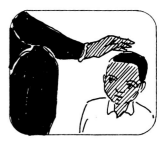

S. puts hand on Boy's head.

Knife moves slightly into frame.

Mary Peer plays the lady in a black leotard who crawls onstage in Act II (among other parts), and she is famous in the group for never getting anywhere on time. She and Wilson had a row about this during rehearsals for the *Stalin* play, as a result of which she did not appear on opening night, but they made it up in time for the three remaining performances. "I don't know what I would have done if it hadn't been for Bob," she says. "I remember one of those early classes of his at the Art Center—he turned the lights down very low and put a record on, and said just do anything you feel like doing. What a wonderful thing! I found myself just sort of tilting, very gradually, down to the floor and going into a somersault. It was the most natural thing in the world. I guess that was about the happiest time of my life, talking to all those different people and learning how to move." Mrs. Peer's husband was a well-to-do lawyer. He died some years ago, and she lives alone in Summit, in a big house by a pond.

Alma Hamilton, Wilson's grandmother, looks in at the

Storyboards for the video adaptation of **I Was Sitting On My Patio This Guy Appeared I Thought I Was Hallucinating**; illustrations by Thomas Woodruff, 1981

Cube rising.

Shutters begin to open.

Cube surfacing on water.

Shutters open.

Cube floating on water surface.

Deck comes out.

dressing-room door, and is invited to come and sit down. She reminisces a bit about Bob. "He was such an interesting child," she says. "I used to take him on all kinds of trips with me, and when he was ten years old he was as good company as any adult." Mrs. Hamilton has always loved to travel. Her husband died fifty years ago, and until quite recently she used to go around by herself on long-distance buses; she has visited every state in the Union and a number of foreign countries. "They used to say my middle name was Goin'," she says, "because I was always goin' somewhere." Now she travels with her grandson and the Byrd Hoffman School. She went with them a year ago to Copenhagen, where she made her theatrical début. "When Bob wants you to do something," she explains, "you just can't get around him." Before the opening in Copenhagen, Wilson asked her whether she thought she could scream onstage. "I said no, but then he sort of demonstrated what he meant, and I tried it. I was just *amazed* at what came out. Who'd have thought my voice could fill a whole theater?"

ACT V
THE TEMPLE

A French critic coined the term "silent opera" to describe Wilson's theater. Others have often suggested that his work is really closer to dance than to anything else—a view to which Wilson himself inclines. Act V is all dance—a free-form, self-taught kind of dancing that grew out of Wilson's body-movement classes and out of the hours and hours of free dancing in the Spring Street loft. Andy de Groat has carried this technique (or non-technique) further than anyone else, and Act V is Andy's act. Wilson has tried hard to stay out of its direction, and he has almost succeeded.

A compact, small-boned young man with close-cropped dark hair, Andy de Groat was going to art school in the daytime and working nights as house manager of the Bleecker Street Cinema when Wilson did a performance there with Kenneth King and others in 1967. They became friends immediately. The following year, Andy performed in *Byrdwoman* and *Alley Cats,* and found his interest shifting, as Wilson's had, from painting to theater. Aside from a few months' work in California with the choreographer Ann Halprin, he has had no formal dance training. "All my dancing is connected with Bob's work," he has said. "I've got something from watching Merce Cunningham and Kenneth King and a few others, but basically it's just from working with Bob and on my own."

Andy de Groat can do things that astonish professional dancers. He can spin for long periods without getting dizzy, turning so rapidly that his body becomes a blur; he can also change direction in midspin, apparently without coming to a stop. His five-minute spin as Heavyman in Act I, where he wears three ape suits under his white costume to pad it out, always evokes applause; during a performance in Paris, he spun continuously for an hour. He knew nothing about whirling dervishes or Sufi mystics when he started doing this, but recently he said that for him spinning "concerns the mind state between waking and sleeping, life and dream, the conscious and the unconscious." He is phenomenally agile, quick, and sure in his movements, and his stage presence is very clear and strong.

Until the production of *Deafman Glance,* Wilson's theater was largely static—a succession of tableaux and very slow movements. The group used dancing only to warm up during rehearsals—to free the body and to get rid of tensions. Since *Deafman,* though, dancing has become much more important. Every Thursday evening at the loft, and before each rehearsal when a play is being prepared, the group dances to records for an hour or more—each person dancing separately, with varying degrees of concentration. Wilson himself, for the last year or so, has been evolving a kind of movement that looks almost spastic in its stumbling lurches and off-balance recoveries. "I hate it," he said sheepishly after rehearsal one day. "If I were in the audience, I wouldn't want to watch anything like that. But I can't seem to stop doing it." His angular, big-footed movements are arresting onstage, and others in the group have obviously been influenced by them. Many more have been influenced by Andy de Groat's spinning, and spins of one sort or another are the basis of much free dancing at the loft. Scotty Snyder, who is rather large, spins slowly and thoughtfully, seldom varying her tempo. Kit Cation (in her twenties) spins very fast, with metronomic precision. Ritty Burchfield and Robyn Anderson and Liz Pasquale and Julia Busto have all developed individual variations of spinning—movements of the arms and the head and the upper body—that seem expressive of their different natures.

This is the raw material that Andy de Groat has used and shaped in his choreography for Act V. The broad patterns have been intricately planned and endlessly rehearsed. Igor Demjen's repetitive, Balinese sounding music, the nearly constant spinning movement of the dancers in their white dresses, and the set itself, which resembles a crypt in an Egyptian pyramid, all trend to suggest some sort of Eastern ritual or temple dance. And yet the dancers themselves seem loose and free, and each moves in a different idiom.

"Maybe the most important thing we've done is to put across this sense of individual vocabularies of movement," Wilson said reflectively one day, over a sandwich in a restaurant across the street from the loft. "I keep thinking about Isadora Duncan—that thing she said about teaching the children in her school not to imitate her movements but to develop the movements that were natural to each one. Isadora was so far ahead of her time—we still haven't caught up with her. Ideally, I guess, what we'd like to do onstage is to present ourselves. Each one presenting himself individually, and at the same time trying to be aware as much as possible of what's happening as a whole group. Not trying to design it or anything—just trying to be aware of it."

There were a lot of problems with Act V in rehearsal. Wilson wanted to leave the direction entirely up to Andy, but was nervous about the way the act seemed to be shaping up. He felt that the stage was getting too crowded. He also thought that several members of the group were not dancing well—that they seemed "jammed up" in their movement and lacking in concentration. "When you come offstage, even for a moment, don't make contact with anybody in the wings," he told them at the end of one unsatisfactory rehearsal. "The main thing is to keep your concentration. You've got to be able to see with your body, in all directions, and to be aware of

everything else that's happening onstage." It was hard for Wilson not to get involved in the details. But every time he made a criticism or a suggestion, he worried afterward that he was undercutting Andy's authority or Andy's confidence. Andy never seemed in the least upset by this. "Everything here comes out of Bob or through Bob," he said cheerfully one afternoon. "What I'm mainly interested in is that people dance well."

While the dancers weave their patterns onstage in Act V, Stalin sits at stage right in an upright rectangular glass box, occasionally speaking into a microphone. For the first part of the act, the Stalin is Wilson. After a time, he is replaced by George Ashley. Ashley has dug up an authentic essay of Stalin's on dialectical and historical materialism, which he reads with deliberation, first in its normal word order and then backward. (Ashley claims that it makes as good sense either way.) He also reads two Emily Dickinson poems, which he chose because they seemed to have some bearing on the life of Stalin. "Bob told me he wanted a Stalin who was dignified, pedantic, infantile, and Chaplinesque," Ashley confided to another member of the cast. "It's clearly impossible, but I do my best."

ENTR'ACTE

Sue Sheehy, her blond hair in curlers, appears in front of the house curtain pushing a heavily laden shopping cart. As she crosses, she tells the audience a story—a true story about an incident in the office of the United Jewish Appeal, where Sue does secretarial work five days a week. It is not a very interesting story, but that doesn't much matter. Watching Sue cross the stage at three-thirty in the morning is not without interest.

There is not the slightest doubt in Sue's mind that she would still be working at Henry's Beef-n-Burger in Iowa City if Robert Wilson and John d'Arcangelo had not come in and spoken to her. There was something

Stations, an original work for video
produced by The Byrd Hoffman
Foundation, the Institut National
d'Audiovisuel, and the Zweites
Deutsches Fernsehen, 1981

86 about this good-natured, heavy girl
which interested them—"the direct
way she shows you just exactly what
she's feeling at that moment" is how
Wilson once put it. As a girl born and
raised in New Sharon, Iowa, Sue had
her moments of doubt, but once she
had performed in *Deafman Glance*
at the university, and Wilson had
praised her performance and
suggested that she come East to be
in the play, the decision was not
difficult. "It was really amazing how
Bob could get what he wanted," Sue
wrote in an autobiographical account
of the experience. "He conveys faith
and trust. You didn't, and I still
don't, question what he asks you to
do." At any rate, Sue bought a
round-trip bus ticket and came to
New York that winter. Never having
been to a major city before, she was
somewhat apprehensive, but Wilson
and Mel Andringa met her at the
Port Authority Bus Terminal (they
had dressed up in ape suits for the
occasion), and a week later she
cashed in her return ticket. In the
summer of 1973, she went back to
Iowa for the first time in almost
three years. It was a mistake, she
found. New York is her home now;
she even likes the subway. She has
played many different roles in
Wilson's plays, and, in addition, she
has become the company's wardrobe
mistress. She has been to Paris and
Copenhagen and Venice, and she has
talked with a princess in Iran.
"People ask me what we're doing—
what it means," she said last winter.
"I say, 'I can't possibly tell you.' But
I like doing it—this is what I want to
do."

ACT VI
THE VICTORIAN BEDROOM

The program says, "Some elements
of music, movement and libretto in
this act were first seen in *KA
MOUNTAIN AND GUARDenia
TERRACE: A Story About a Family
and Some People Changing*,
presented at the Festival of Arts,
Shiraz-Persepolis, Iran, in 1972."

Fifteen members of the Byrd
Hoffman School went to France with
Wilson in the spring of 1972 to
conduct a theater workshop that was
sponsored jointly by Jean-Louis
Barrault's Théâtre des Nations and
Michel Guy's Festival d'Automne.
The material developed at the
workshop would be presented at the
Shiraz Festival, to which they had
been invited by the Iranian
government. They spent six weeks in
a lovely thirteenth-century abbey at
Royaumont, about an hour from
Paris, living and working with

professional French actors and
dancers whom Wilson had selected
through a series of auditions. Alone
or in small groups, they wrote plays,
made dances, painted and constructed
sets. In June, the Wilson group
dispersed to various parts of Europe,
prior to reassembling in Iran. Wilson,
Andy de Groat, Ann Wilson (a
painter, Willard Gallery; no relation),
and Kit Cation went to Crete, where
Wilson's European agent and friend,
Ninon Tallon Karlweis, had offered to
let them use her house. After a week
of relaxation, they were on the point
of leaving for Iran when a customs

officer at the airport in Heraklion found a small parcel of hashish in Wilson's coat pocket. The next five weeks were a nightmare for everyone concerned. Wilson was arrested on the spot, searched (they found nothing more), and imprisoned without bail. For the next few days, Andy de Groat and George Ashley, who was in Shiraz with the rest of the company, spent most of their time on the telephone to Paris and New York, where influential friends were trying to find the right strings to pull. A local lawyer who had been engaged to represent Wilson told them that the best he could hope for was a trial in six months and a one-year jail sentence, and that it could be much worse. After five weeks, and against the lawyer's advice, Andy again applied for bail, and, to everyone's surprise, it was granted—with the stern warning that under no circumstances was Wilson to leave Greece. Wilson and the others flew immediately to Athens, took the first non-Greek flight they could find, and held their breath until they landed in Istanbul. He has since heard that he has been amnestied by the new Greek government, but he does not intend to visit the country again for some time.

In Shiraz, meanwhile, Ashley had kept the company going as best he could. Nearly everyone had been hospitalized at least once for dehydration—the temperature got up to about a hundred and twenty degrees every day—and the festival authorities, in Wilson's absence, were extremely chary with funds. Although a month had been lost, Wilson managed to pull together the Royaumont material and to generate enough new material for *Overture*, a one-hour play presented in the garden of a famous house in Shiraz, and for *KA MOUNTAIN AND GUARDenia TERRACE*, which lasted, in the land of Scheherazade, for seven days and seven nights. *KA MOUNTAIN* began ("opened" hardly seems the word) at

midnight on September 2nd in Shiraz, at the foot of a hill called Haft-tan, or Seven Bodies, in reference to the graves of seven Sufi poets buried there. Each day thereafter, the performers moved to an area higher on the mountain, reaching the summit for the seventh and last day's performance. In the intervals between the main passages, there were continuous activities on a platform near the foot of the mountain. A detailed program showed what was happening each day, and where, and for how long.

What *was* happening? Dozens of individual plays, dances, pantomimes, and tableaux that had been developed by various members of the company —the program listed seventeen directors and nine authors and a cast of seventy-nine (the majority of whom were students at Pahlavi University in Shiraz). The first night's audience included the flower of Iranian society, in mink stoles and precipitous high heels. Within an hour, the élite had departed (they evidently were expecting a traditional opera), and their places were taken by students, who came equipped for the chilly night air with blankets, foodstuffs, and stimulants. There was an audience of some kind in attendance for a good part of the hundred-and-sixty-eight-hour performance, except during the torrid hours between noon and 3 P.M. Life is a good deal slower in Iran than it is in New York, and the play's length caused little public outrage. "There were times, though, when nobody was watching us," Wilson recalls. "At three in the afternoon, with the sun overhead, everybody except us was home sleeping. It made me wonder about the difference between living and performing. *KA MOUNTAIN* in some ways was like a documentation of what we're like— we were the family and the people changing. I think it's a piece I could work on for the rest of my life."

Several members of the group went through crises of one sort or another during or soon after *KA MOUNTAIN*. Scotty Snyder contracted typhoid and pneumonia, and spent two weeks in a hospital in Shiraz. George Ashley and Anna-Lisa Larsdotter stayed with her while the others went on to Paris, where they had been invited to give a performance at the Festival d'Automne, and where Cindy Lubar—a tower of strength all through the Shiraz experience—began to show some alarming symptoms. Normally a quiet and rather withdrawn girl, Cindy became very aggressive during the Paris rehearsals, ordering others around in a loud voice and repeating words compulsively. She could not sit still for a moment. One day, she came to rehearsal in a bright-red dress and silver shoes, with her dark hair bleached white-blond. The next morning, she showed up with her head shaved. Wilson and the others were in a quandary. They thought that if they took her to a doctor she would be institutionalized, and those in the group who had had experience with mental institutions thought anything would be preferable to that. Wilson finally got through to her. He told her to take a week off and sleep, which is what she did.

Cindy talks freely about the experience now. "I felt as though too many things were happening in my mind at the same time," she said last winter. "It was interesting, but I was scared, too, because it was so out of control. I'm terrifically grateful that I was with the group, because otherwise I know I would have gone to a mental hospital, and I might still be there. People like Bob and Ann Wilson made me feel it was all right, what was happening to me."

Cindy, it seems, was then able to put what had happened to her into *Ouverture,* a twenty-four-hour Wilson opus at the Opéra-Comique that became, in effect, Cindy's play. "She was onstage nearly the whole time," Mel Andringa recalls. "Sometimes she slept onstage. For hours at a time, she would do those queer, broken vocalizations of hers, and you never knew when she might go out of control completely. It was painful to watch, but absolutely compelling. At the end, she took off her coat—she was nude underneath—knelt down, and started to wash her hands and arms in a pool of water that was onstage. The lighting was exceptionally beautiful just then. It was incredibly moving—you felt as though she had come through it and out the other side."

The Theater of Madness has its historical antecedents, including the Marquis de Sade's Charenton productions and the currently influential writings of Antonin Artaud. Wilson's willingness to incorporate individual breakdowns into his theater pieces—to allow for the occurrence of breakdowns, if not actually to provoke them—may represent a further step in this direction, and a step that raises some fairly heavy questions. When asked about it recently, Wilson said that Cindy's breakdown, Francine Felgeirolles's instability, and the fact that others in the group often seemed to be close to the edge mentally or emotionally concerned him a great deal, but that it also seemed important to him to explore the kinds of communication that such states opened up. People like Francine and Christopher Knowles, he said, were acutely sensitive to all forms of nonverbal communication, and they seemed to respond in a good way to being placed in a theatrical situation or environment. Theater itself, Wilson said, was a kind of organized insanity. Jerome Robbins has put the matter in much the same way. "Bob is attracted, somewhat, to what the rest of us would consider the misfits of this world. He sees in them the exceptional," he said not long ago. "This is part of his caring. Theater is all a little crazy anyway. After all, what could be madder than a lot of people in ballet shoes dancing on their toes? We're apt to say the new thing is the maddest, because we're not used to it, but maybe his work is saner than anything else around. One of Bob's great contributions is another way of looking at the

Preliminary sketches and rehearsal
for **Medea**, an opera with music by
Gavin Bryars, Kennedy Center for
the Performing Arts, Washington,
D.C., 1981

90 question 'What is theater?' What he does is make you think about the whole question. And I firmly believe that his contribution will be as great as that of any theater man in America."

The madness in Act VI, at any rate, is not very upsetting. There are twelve beds onstage, and twelve sleepers in white nightgowns and white mobcaps, and an old man with a staff who laboriously counts to ten, and, behind him, an octagonal, mirrored room through which various characters make stealthy entrances and exits. The sleepers get up every so often and search with lanterns for an invisible "thief." Queen Victoria appears, to announce that "conflict in the created world is not what it seems," but Stalin is nowhere in sight. The act goes on rather too long, and, coming at the time it does —between three-thirty and four-fifteen in the morning—and considering the imagery, it provides an almost irresistible invitation to nap. Nobody leaves the theater at this hour. Wintry gusts can be heard buffeting the Academy walls, and there are few taxis at 4 A.M. The bedroom setting and the lighting are eminently restful. One dozes. One wakes briefly to see Sheryl Sutton, in a white satin suit, doing a music-hall turn. One dozes again. The dream continues.

ENTR'ACTE

The raised platform is a black lake ringed with icebergs. Kit Cation plays the flute at stage right. Julia Busto, wearing a man's dark suit and a fedora, dances among the icebergs. (She will remain on the platform throughout Act VII, turning continuously in slow, smooth circles, never varying her tempo.)

Behind the house curtain, the cast again forms a circle, hands linked. Wilson, who posted a notice backstage an hour ago ("Circle of hands before Act VII—everyone"), stands in the center. He thanks them all for their work and says he thinks the play is going well tonight. Act VII, he says, is the most difficult act

of all—the one that has given the most trouble in rehearsal. "I've been worried about people holding back in this act," he says. "But maybe all the trouble we've had in rehearsal came from my trying to make it into something it isn't. Maybe Cindy and the others are right to hold back. There's a point of saturation for the audience. Well, O.K. Let's have a good show."

ACT VII
THE PLANET

Ostriches fill the stage. Thirty-two of them, turning and bowing and strutting stiff-legged in a stately ostrich ballet—choreography by Mel Andringa and Andy de Groat, music by Alan Lloyd. The costumes are marvels. Although the bare legs are clearly human, the large feathered bodies and the towering necks and beaks and the queer hopping movements create an uncanny illusion. Their dance is a counterpart to the dance of the sixty mammies in Act I—one of many correspondences. Act I ties up with Act VII, Act II with Act VI, Act III with Act V, while Act IV stands alone at the center. Now, as in Act I, the stage is covered with sand (which the ostriches kick up), and most of the characters who appeared in the first act will reappear in the last.

The new element in Act VII—the element that has made it, for Wilson, more difficult and more interesting than the other acts—is language. Once the ostriches have made their exit, the act is peopled by characters who actually recite lines, though rarely to one another. This is a new direction in Wilson's work, which in the past has been largely nonverbal. To a certain extent, of course, language has been an element in all six of the previous acts, what with Stalin explaining dialectical materialism and Queen Victoria holding forth on pineal movements and a chorus whose members talk Parsi or say "click" and "collect." In Act VII, however, language becomes the central element, although not in

Jessye Norman in **Great Day in the Morning**, Théâtre des Champs-Elysées, Paris, 1982

precisely the same sense as the language in a Neil Simon play.

Until Wilson was seventeen, he had a severe speech impediment. "I had great difficulty getting anything out," he said once. "But just as I was graduating from high school I met this amazing person—the dancer who was working with brain-damaged children in Texas. She said, 'Oh, you can speak.' I don't even think it was what she said as much as the way she said it. Within three months, I was making lots of progress. Part of it was just slowing down. I learned to speak very, very slowly. I entered a radio speaking contest, and spoke very slowly over the air—it became funny, and then it became theatrical, a sort of projected image. It was a very important Thant time for me, like a dam bursting."

The use of language in *The Life and Times of Joseph Stalin* seems to be another kind of breakthrough for Wilson, and it will be interesting to see how this develops in his future work. At the moment, language is something he uses as another theatrical material, like movement or light; the sense of the words is of minor importance. Listening to the sounds that Raymond Andrews and Cindy Lubar made in his classes started Wilson thinking about the relation between sound and movement, and this, in turn, led to some odd experiments. In 1971, Wilson gave a "press conference" in Yugoslavia in which he simply repeated the word "dinosaur" over and over, for twelve hours, while cutting an onion the whole time. "Students and other people would come up and ask why I kept saying 'dinosaur,' and I'd keep saying

'Dinosaur Dinosaur Dinosaur,' and after a while I'd feel as though I had answered their question. I suppose the idea is that we already know the answers to most of our questions. I wasn't sure whether or not I was actually *saying* other words, but I knew I was *hearing* other words, like 'disaster' and 'soaring.' It's very curious. Anyway, the object of a lot of the work we're doing with movement is to break movements down into very small units. Like Balinese dancers, who have something like a hundred and seventy-five eye movements alone. The question becomes 'Can we break down the phrasing of sounds in the same way, and work with that?' You notice in the *Stalin* script we say 'O.K.' a lot. 'O.K. O.K. O.K. O.K. O.K. O.K.' Sometimes I feel that the emotions can shift more rapidly when we do this than when we talk as we ordinarily do. We also say 'Hmm' a lot. It's amazing how often people do that in conversation. It communicates something about all sorts of other things that are happening besides the words. Also, it's international—it's understood in Paris or Copenhagen or anywhere. We were invited to do a radio program on WBAI—a five-hour program, from midnight to 5 A.M. It didn't work out too well. My idea was to do the program in three parts. The first part would be a group of us saying 'Hmm' in all sorts of different ways; in the second part we'd say 'O.K.;' and in the third part we'd say 'There.' 'There There There There There.' I thought it would be nice if some truck driver turned on the radio late at night and got a bunch of people going 'Hmm' or 'There.' But the program manager wasn't too happy, and she kept asking questions

Sketches for **Parsifal**, an opera by
Richard Wagner, 1982

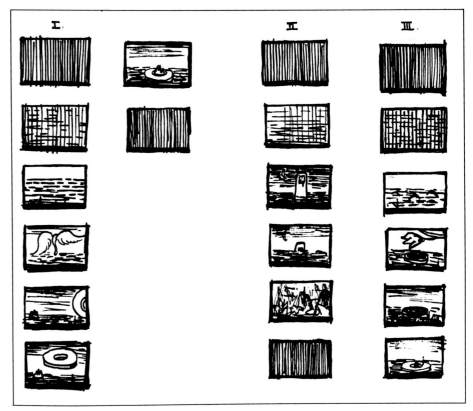

that weren't very interesting. Why do
people ask such uninteresting
questions? My grandmother is close
to ninety, and she's never once asked
me what the play means or why
people are going around in it without
their clothes on. Most of the
important things never get
communicated in words anyway.''

The backdrop for Act VII is a
landscape on the moon, or some less
familiar planet. The red runner
passes in the deepest zone, and Julia
Busto turns and turns on the
downstage platform. A pair of
tourists appear, outlandishly garbed;
the man takes a photograph of a
hole. Smoke comes from the hole, and
then Sheryl Sutton, reciting a speech
from *Medea*. Stagehands drag in a
platform bearing four people: a man
who holds a quizzing glass to his eye
and intones cosmic news reports, a
woman who reads from a book, a
man with a tree on his head, and
Queen Victoria, who paces restlessly
back and forth. Their voices
sometimes combine and overlap,

sometimes fall silent. The man with
the tree on his head is Stefan Brecht,
who writes on theater (his wife,
Mary, designed the costumes for this
play, among others); he was also the
red-haired waiter in Act IV, and the
old man who counts to ten in Act VI.
Stefan is the son of Bertolt Brecht,
who almost certainly would not have
approved of Robert Wilson. Stefan
reads from a Ford Foundation report,
from the Book of Job, from *Gestes et
Opinions du Docteur Faustroll*, by
Alfred Jarry. Other familiar figures
come and go: Freud and Anna, Ivan
the Terrible, the dancing Heavyman.
Wilhelm Reich is dragged offstage by
two vigilantes shouting ''Communist!''
A man in a long fur coat comes on
carrying two large blocks of ice.
Slides of a closing door are projected.
High up in the darkened sky, a shape
like a spiral nebula glows luminously,
outlining the figures of a bride and
groom. The bride appears to be
strangling the groom, but without
violence. A winged horse flies across
the sky. The lights come up onstage,
the nebula fades out, and another
cycle of action begins.

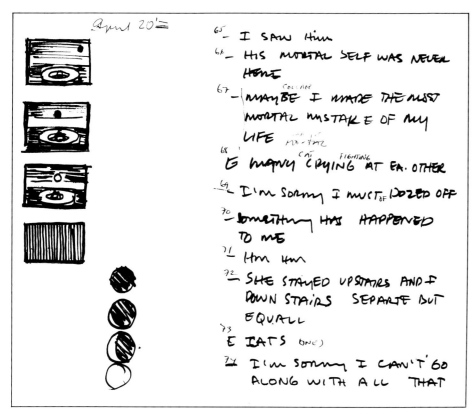

There are about four hundred people left in the audience, some of them asleep. "Sometimes people go to sleep and see things that aren't there," Wilson says. "When you have a group of people together for twelve hours or twenty-four hours, all sorts of things happen. The brain begins to operate on a slower frequency. Ideally, in our work, someone in the audience might reach a point of consciousness where he is on the same frequency as one of the performers—where he receives communications directly."

Time passes. The man with the melting blocks of ice says, "It won't be long now." Ann Wilson, the woman reading the book on the platform, recites a speech that Wilson wrote five years ago—a sort of prologue to *The Life and Times of Sigmund Freud.* She has a lovely, strong voice, and she reads it beautifully:

And now in saying something, something introductory to get something settled or someone adjusted there is going on and getting started.

ON WITH THE SHOW! as they used to say in the days that I like to remember when people used to waltz. And when they square danced. And when they sat in drawing rooms and played pianos gently to themselves. Then it all changed. Someone got an idea. Things were never the—no, no I won't say it but, then I see in the same pictures and in the flood of encoding the detail the voices of beasts the power coming over the walls through the memory as they do slicing the onion the man into (his) particulars and appearing as they do on the trail of a voice singing a void arresting a beach dissolving through his ears of the cave.

"It won't be long now," says the iceman.

In the distant sky, where the nebula glows, the city of Moscow is in flames. A ragged mob in thick military overcoats thunder across the stage. They are stopped with a gesture by Stalin—a slim Stalin (Sheryl Sutton this time) in military green. A telephone rings onstage. Stalin answers it ("This is Joseph Stalin"), and expresses mild surprise that an aide will not speak up for a friend who is about to be shot. Stalin climbs a flight of stairs and stands looking down on the motionless crowd. A bassoon sounds. Violin and flute take up the accompaniment, and the crowd starts to hum a Baroque chorale by the seventeenth-century German composer Pachelbel. Slowly, very slowly, at six-fifty in the morning, the curtain comes down. Everybody is onstage when it comes up again—a hundred and forty-four people plus a few stagehands, who have been pulled there by Wilson and others. The applause sounds tremendous. The cast is applauding back, and then suddenly, in some access of unspent energy, the cast is jumping up and down on the stage, applauding and jumping and raising a great cloud of golden dust as the curtain comes down for the last time.

Robert Wilson: Current Projects
Laurence Shyer,
December 1982

Robert Wilson is in New York on one of his increasingly rare visits. He sits in his loft overlooking the Westside Highway with a cup of tea after a long afternoon of appointments, conferences and phone calls. Although it is Sunday, it is a working day like every other. Outside, snow is banked against the industrial buildings and warehouses of Tribeca, and across the Hudson, the drab industrial skyline of New Jersey can be seen in the waning light of a December day. The large, spare interior of Wilson's loft offers a striking contrast to the cold and creeping darkness below. Clear glass lightbulbs suspended overhead cast a uniform brightness over the open space with its white walls, clean gray floors and small groupings of minimalist furniture. Some of the walls are covered with Wilson's graphite sketches for his latest spectacle, row upon row of neat little rectangles which combine to form larger geometric patterns. Even in its present disarray, the room suggests the aesthetic concerns of its creator: care, simplicity, order and the controlled, almost severe disposition of elements. (It is interesting that the loft residence of Richard Foreman, America's other major avant-garde theater artist, also seems to personify his work: dark, alienating, somewhat seedy and sinister.)

This trip, like most of Wilson's other New York visits, is a stopover. Only last week he was in Los Angeles soliciting support for his newest and most ambitious opera, *the CIVIL warS*. The previous day was spent conferring with technicians from Munich, and soon he will leave to supervise a showing of his drawings at the Rhode Island School of Design in Providence. He has had little sleep in the last three days and it shows.

All of which is to say that Robert Wilson is in demand—though less in his own country than around the world. Not one of the new works he has created in Europe over the past five years has been performed in the United States; in fact, American audiences have not seen a large-scale Wilson work since *Einstein on the*

Beach was presented at the Metropolitan Opera House in 1976. Since that time they have had to content themselves with chamber pieces such as *DIA LOG/Curious George,* which was produced at Lincoln Center three years ago, and a number of workshops or "open rehearsals." (Wilson's scenery and lighting for Lucinda Child's dance piece *Relative Calm* were also seen at the Brooklyn Academy of Music in 1981.)

With *the CIVIL warS* under way, Wilson has become more than ever an international entity, flying from country to country, his far-flung itinerary determined by commissions, funding, and a desire to win new audiences. At the offices of his Byrd Hoffman Foundation on Spring Street, administrators and assistants scurry from meeting to meeting pursuing funding sources and organizing the details of his career. Robert Wilson has become a small industry.

For Wilson, time has also become an increasingly precious commodity, something to be carefully allotted and used to maximum effect. His schedule, finalized months in advance, fills a loose-leaf binder. As a result, arranging an appointment or an interview with Wilson is likely to be a wearing ritual of confirmations, cancellations and delays. As the director of his foundation says, it's almost easier to see the President.

Here in his own loft, amid his white walls and his graphite drawings, Wilson is a study of changing moods and attitudes; alternately laconic and talkative, languorous and passionate, dreamy and direct. He is also unfailingly polite and, in an odd way, even charming—the genuineness of his sudden swoops of laughter and periodic bursts of enthusiasm positively disarm one. While one gets a sense of his celebrated personal magnetism, what doesn't really show in casual conversation is his terrific force of will—the most remarkable thing about Wilson, after all, is not his art so much as his unfailing ability to make it happen.

Preliminary sketches for the
"Epilogue to Act Four," **the CIVIL
warS**, 1982

I,A

Knee Play 1:
-Man in a tree
-A lion underneath the tree
-Silent
-Man in tree is hanging
-Goethe on a table,
-Flying vultures

Huge Map of a Continent
-Two people making chart
-Village of Berlin/Brandenburg
 Gate in miniature Downstage
-Ladders start to dance
-Light signs on the wall

-Radio speech,Henry V(tape)
-Tin soldier,mechanical doll,
 drummer boy
-Continent splits in two
-Thallis-like music
-View of Gedachtnis-Church,Berlin,
 some fat rabbits

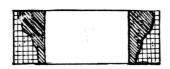

-Lonesome marching soldier
-Other towers appear
-Wind grows out of music

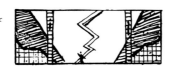

-Grey sky
-Voltaire enters through trap door
 in yellow light
-Orchestra comes up in pit
-Voltaire,Frederick the Great

-Marching soldiers in red uniforms
-Frederick the Great
-Continent splits into parts

I,B

Knee Play 2:
-Two men have cut down tree
-Tree falls slowly
-Men carry tree off,they return
 with a log.
-With another person,they attach
 log to a cabin.

Winter:snowing
-Civil War soldier,whistling,
 begins to cross SR-SL
-Old Lady comes out of a house
 and tends garden
-Mata Hari skates along canal,
 other skaters pass

Snow lightens
-World's Tallest Woman enters SR:
 she carries a tiny man on her
 hand(William the Silent).
-Civil War soldier still crossing

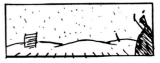

-Tallest Woman sets down small man
 on a coffin.
-Ice skaters skate,remove skates
 and walk off.
-Old Woman tends garden,
 soldier still crossing

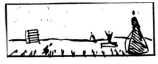

Autumn
-Soldier crossing,Woman in garden,
 Tallest woman crossing stage
-Scything
-Others work in field
-Haystacks

-Harvest Dance
-Boy with cow enters SR

Summer
-Soldier still crossing
-Tallest Woman center stage
-A boat sails along canal
-Boy says farewell to old man and
 woman,exits SL with cow

In the course of the following conversation, Wilson discusses his recent European productions and a number of upcoming projects, also touching on such subjects as his current collaborations and his continued absence from this country. While Wilson tends to weigh his thoughts carefully and answer methodically, he does not always answer a question directly; often he seizes on an aspect that interests him or steers the inquiry in a direction that does, or something else occurs to him and he goes that way. He seems most comfortable describing his designs and the action of his pieces or relating the formative experiences and the familiar artistic perceptions that one finds in most of his interviews. Should the conversation turn toward matters of intention or meaning, he is likely to become inarticulate, impatient or weary. Wilson, incidentally, possesses something of the storyteller's art, the ability to fascinate and carry the listener along regardless of what he is saying, and sadly this loses a certain amount in transcription. As Wilson speaks about his work, he often illustrates his ideas on a small sketch pad ("I doodle constantly, I doodle [a design] so many times it's in my body," he recently told a correspondent for the International *Herald-Tribune*).

I,B(cont):

-Tallest Woman;soldier crossing.
-Boy returns with beans,speaks
 with old man who throws away
 beans.

-Beanstalk grows
-Boy runs to and climbs beanstalk
-Old Woman in garden.

-Old Woman in Garden
-Soldier still crossing
-Duet between Boy on beanstalk
 and Tallest Woman.
-Old Man watches.

Blackout.

Giants'house in sky(possibly film)
-Boy enters on tiptoe,hides in
 cupboard
-Giant enters and sits at table.
-Giantess enters with food and
 spies boy

-Giants eat
-Boy finds harp in cupboard and
 begins to play.
-Giants go to investigate
-Boy with harp runs off.

Spring
-Civil War soldier crossing
-Old Man and Woman in garden
-Tallest Woman SL
-Boy climbs down beanstalk
-Large bird flies through sky

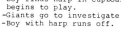

I,B (cont.)

-Boy cuts down beanstalk and
 Giant falls into tulip garden

-Boy moves SL and plays harp
-Mata Hari enters from house and
 walks DS
-Civil War soldier crosses
 stage and exits SL.

You've just returned from Paris where you produced *Great Day in the Morning,* an evening of Negro spirituals, with the celebrated American soprano Jessye Norman. In the summer of 1984, Norman will also be appearing in your staging of *the CIVIL warS.* How did this ongoing collaboration come about?

About five years ago I was performing in Paris and Jessye was there singing at the same time. She's a big, big star in France, much bigger than she is in America. Various people had told me that I would like what she was doing so I went to one of her performances and I was overwhelmed by her—by the way she walked on stage, the way she stood and, of course, the way she sang. With the least amount of effort she can fill an enormous hall. That's Jessye's genius. She can sing the quietest, softest sound with her back to the audience and that sound will touch the back wall of the theater. So I was overwhelmed and I went backstage and stood in line and said, "Hello, my name is Bob Wilson. You're absolutely fantastic and I would love to work with you." She didn't know who I was and asked, "What is it that you do?" "Well, I'm a theater director and artist. I make works for the theater." "Well," she said, "thank you very much" and that was it. Then about eight months later I was in Texas visiting my family and I read in a Dallas paper that she was appearing at Tanglewood. I was coming back to New York anyway so I decided to go straight to Tanglewood and hear her sing. Again, I was overwhelmed. I went backstage and stood in a long line and finally when my turn came, she turned and said, "Oh, hello, Mr. Wilson, it's nice to see you again." She has a phenomenal memory. Anyway, we had lunch the next day and I told her about a new piece that I was going to do in Berlin (*Death, Destruction and Detroit*). I made some drawings for her and tried to explain how I work. Then I told her that when I do the piece I would like her to come and see it. And she did come. Soon after that I began to make sketches and work on an idea

I,C

II,A

Knee Play 3:
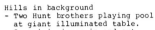
- Two men build a boat hull

Knee Play 4:
- Three people finish building
  boat;they push it to water.
- Another person enters with drink
  and they christen the boat.
- They sail off in boat.

-Two tigers in hills(puppets,
 being worked by two women)
-They sing Japanese poems

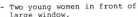

- Two young women in front of
  large window.
- Through window can be seen
  escalators with people moving up
  and down.

Hills in background
- Two Hunt brothers playing pool
  at giant illuminated table.
- One ninja jumps in and out.

- Two old women on either side of
  stage.Dialogue.

Pool table splits into two tables:
- At one,two Hunt brothers
- At other,Minamoto no Yoritomo
  and Yoshitsune.
- Three ninjas jump in and out.

- General Lee's horse on stage
  for two minutes.
- Music.

Pool tables remain.
- Two giraffes and two tigers.
- Tigers sing, Giraffes speak.

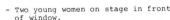

- Two young women on stage in front
  of window.
- Two old women on either side of
  stage. Dialogue.

- Two tigers, two giraffes.
- Eight pool tables with two
  Hunts,Two Minamoto brothers,
  six other pairs.
-Tigers sing,Giraffes speak,
 people sing;many different languages.
- Suddenly they all sing together
  in Japanese and the earth appears
  in the distance.

-Two young women and two old women.
-General Lee on skeleton of horse.

- Two tigers and eight pool tables.
- Tigers crawl down from mountains
  and go under pool tables to sing.

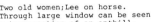
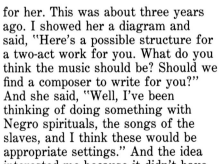

-Two old women;Lee on horse.
-Through large window can be seen
 a transsection of an anthill.

END OF ACT ONE.

for her. This was about three years ago. I showed her a diagram and said, "Here's a possible structure for a two-act work for you. What do you think the music should be? Should we find a composer to write for you?" And she said, "Well, I've been thinking of doing something with Negro spirituals, the songs of the slaves, and I think these would be appropriate settings." And the idea interested me because it didn't have anything to do with slavery necessarily, it wouldn't have to be an illustration of the music—you know, a black person in a field of cotton. So Jessye and I began talking and thinking about what songs to use and how they should be fitted together.

We began a collaboration. Over the last two years we'd get together from time to time and rehearse and gradually we found what the piece was about. It was a very close collaboration. I really think I work best when I can build and create a work with someone.

How would you characterize the relationship between the songs and your own visual presentation?

I just picked settings that I thought were appropriate in some way for this music as a group of pictures or tableaux but which didn't necessarily illustrate the music. And everything had to be in scale to Jessye. There were certain moods in the landscapes

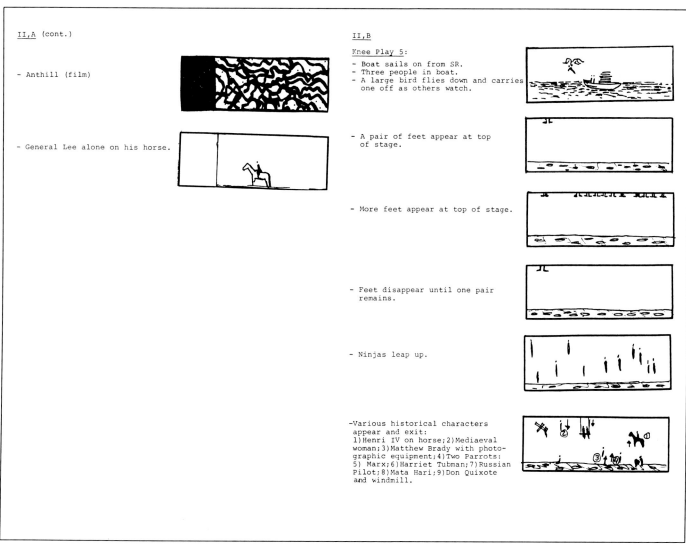

- Anthill (film)

- General Lee alone on his horse.

Knee Play 5:
- Boat sails on from SR.
- Three people in boat.
- A large bird flies down and carries one off as others watch.

- A pair of feet appear at top of stage.

- More feet appear at top of stage.

- Feet disappear until one pair remains.

- Ninjas leap up.

-Various historical characters appear and exit:
1)Henri IV on horse;2)Mediaeval woman;3)Matthew Brady with photographic equipment;4)Two Parrots: 5) Marx;6)Harriet Tubman;7)Russian Pilot;8)Mata Hari;9)Don Quixote and windmill.

---

that helped in deciding what songs to use but the songs are not meant to illustrate the background. The background is like a picture book that makes sense on its own. In *Great Day,* the visual is as important as what we hear. I think it helps us hear and the singing helps us see. I think what I disliked about opera when I first went was that I couldn't hear; I was so visually distracted. I heard best when I shut my eyes. It's very difficult to see and hear at the same time and mostly we do one or the other. What I try to do in all my work is make a balance between what you hear and what you see, so that perhaps you can do both at the same time.

These days your productions are usually greeted with instantaneous acclaim, but *Great Day* created something of a furor at its première in Paris. In fact, you were vigorously booed by a large faction of the audience at the end of the performance. I imagine the presence of Jessye Norman might have attracted a somewhat different audience than usually attends your productions, perhaps one unprepared for the kind of work you do.

I think it's an audience that tends to go to concerts, recitals and opera, not necessarily my audience. She had sung many times at that theater and so a lot of people came expecting the kind of thing they had heard in the past. They also didn't understand what spirituals are. These songs are

religious in nature, they're all from the Bible which was the only book the slaves had to read. They're not songs of anger; they're songs of nobility and dignity, the songs of an oppressed race. The problems resulted from a misunderstanding—audiences not knowing what the spirituals are, not knowing how the music came about or the way it was sung or simply the way it *was,* which was to some extent the way we presented it. They were frustrated and confused. The staging and designs responded to the religious nature of the music and the way the songs were sung. They were sung as a way of life—you heard singing as you woke up in the morning and

II,B (cont)

Historical figures:
  10)Civil War nurse; 11)Angel;
  12)American Indian; 13)Joan of
  Arc;14)Business man.
- A plane flies upside down.

- Gradually most characters exit
  flying upward and down into stage
  floor,leaving Joan of Arc singing,
  a businessman dummy,and a few
  floating characters.

II,C

Knee Play 6:
- The boat is beached on a rock.
- Two people load the boat, then
  write on the hull.

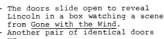

- Two large metal doors.
- Two hysterical opera singers in
  rehearsal clothes, screaming.
- Loud knocking from behind.

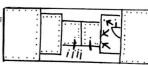

- The doors slide open to reveal
  Lincoln in a box watching a scene
  from Gone with the Wind.
- Another pair of identical doors
  US.
- Singers have moved US.
- Lincoln is shot and begins to
  fall slowly.

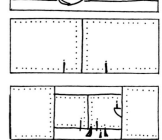

- Second set of doors opens revealing
  the Noh drama Funa Benkei in progress.
- Another set of doors US.
- Noh play freezes;Lincoln continues
  to fall
- Lincoln reaches ground.

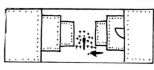

- Third set of doors open to reveal
  Lincoln with back to audience
  addressing crowd US: Gettysburg
  Address

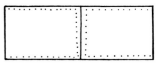

- In middle of Gettysburg Address,
  the DS doors slam shut with a
  loud bang.

- Doors open very slowly to reveal
  two large cliffs.
- Between cliffs, a small boat carrying a giraffe to China(14th C.)
  and Admiral Perry to Japan(19th
  C.)

END OF ACT TWO.

---

dressed, you sang as you went through the day, it was the way you closed the day. Jessye said she always remembered hearing her grandmother sing all day long. Her mother too. The slaves grew up singing as part of life. It was not something they did for entertainment, it was a way of life. It was natural, like breathing. There was song all day long.

And that's actually the form of *Great Day.* It's a kind of progression through the day.

Right, that's it. It's a great day and a woman begins the morning singing. It starts early in the morning with the sunrise and it ends with the morning again. Singing is heard through the course of the day. I show various things that people would do every day. You see someone contemplating and someone walking in a forest.

You see someone waking up in bed and someone sleeping in the middle of the night. I made this room with a huge window.

It's not a specific room or even a window necessarily. It could be 1840 or 2040.

Perhaps you could describe the scene on the lake, which drew praise from critics as well as scornful laughter from some members of the audience. It seems to embody the spiritual nature of the work and the meditative qualities you were seeking to capture.

III,A

Knee Play 7:
- The Boat sails along a coast.
- On shore,two people load a cannon and fire at the boat.
- The boat is hit and breaks up; the hull sinks but the cabin floats on.

- Battle of the Monitor and the Merrimac.

Underwater Scene:

- An old and a young John Wilkes Booth float by in glass boxes.
- Speech

- Blackout

Submarine Window:
- Ox and Nemo look through window at underwater garden.
- Goddess outside.
- Booth in glass case floats by.
- Queen of Sea comes inside through window to Ox and Nemo.

- Madame Curie bicycles from the garden through the window and sits at a desk DS.

- Ox,Nemo,and Mme Curie.

III,A (cont)

-Four Dr Mudds in underwater cages.
-Ox and Nemo look out into garden, but do not see them.

Underwater Ball Scene·
- Staircase of the Paris Opera; Large Portholes on either side.
- All Characters descend stairs.

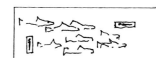

- Queen of the Sea's party.
- Queen greets her guests.
- Mme Curie enters, all others freeze.
- Mme Curie and Queen exit on a bicycle.

- Mme Curie walks into distance and through solid metal doors.
- Dr Mudd follows her.

- Crystal City.
- Booth cases are empty.
- Mme Curie and Mudd walk through the city.

- Booths in glass cases,monsters, and sharks.

There's a dock out in the lake and it's midnight.

There are stars in the sky and the moonlight is reflecting on the water. Jessye walks out in a blue robe and sings a song she wrote herself, a song based on a slave poem that's sung *a cappella*. There's a simple white chair at the end of the dock. She walks over to it and begins to sing "Sometimes I Feel Like a Motherless Child." A little golden light falls down on her as she sits in the white chair improvising the song. She's written a part for a cello and as it's played a gray Canadian goose moves across the sky, its wings slowly flapping. But she doesn't see it, her focus is turned inward. She

has two or three very simple gestures that are counted and carefully lit. After sitting there for ten minutes or so, humming and singing, she stands up and begins to walk off. Just before she gets to the edge of the stage she kneels down and takes a handful of water from the lake and washes her face. And she begins to sing again. Then she turns and walks offstage in profile, humming the same music. And that's how we did these songs. We didn't present them like gospel numbers, adding tambourines and banjos and making an entertainment—all that came later. And so when Jessye was humming a song for ten minutes or sitting in silence the audience became

very restless. But it would have been very inappropriate to present this music any other way and that was completely misunderstood—though not by the serious writers of the French press who did understand for the most part. I must say that I was surprised by the incredible reaction at the end, the bursts of boos and bravos. Some of the press wrote that it was an occasion similar to the première of *The Rite of Spring,* which had its first performance in the same theater over sixty years before. After that, there was no way of ever getting away from the idea of a controversy because audiences came expecting a controversial event and they acted controversial.

III,B

Flower-patterned drop with giant
teacup.
- An elegant Tenth Century Japanese
  court lady announces the wedding
  of the Sun Goddess Ameratsu with
  her Brother in order to produce
  the Japanese Imperial Family.

III,C (cont.)

- Nurses go to beds,remove mosquito
  nets,revealing ten Lincolns,
  one in each bed.
- The various Lincolns act out
  their cartoons:
  Devil; Tightrope walker; Nurse-
  maid; Stickman; Acrobat; Comic;
  Baboon; Black man with veil;
  Scotsman in freight car; Othello.

- Lee in bed.
- Curtain drawn back.
- Projection of burnt out ruins
  of Richmond.
- Marie Curie at desk.

14

III,C

- Large window with curtain
- General Lee in hospital bed.
- Mme Curie at desk.
- Lee's daughter visits.

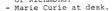

- Lee is dying.
- Members of his family gather
  around his bed: Wife,two sons
  (no epaulettes on shoulders),
  and three daughters.
- Marie Curie speaks.

- Lee in bed.
- Mme Curie leaves.
- Projection of sailboats on
  curtain.

- Lee dies.
- Projection of sailboats
  superimposed over ruins of
  Richmond.
- 24 small children in white
  dresses and pantaloons play
  around Lee on deathbed.

Blackout.

Civil War Hospital;door at center
stage:
- Giant Bee on ceiling.
- Ten army cots with mosquito
  nets,five on each side.
- Six nurses enter through door
  and waltz.

- Mme Curie enters with radium lamp
- Nurses in Victorian uniform dance
  into spaces between beds,Head
  nurse waltzes down center of ward.
- Nurses dance to center,Head nurse
  stands watching them.
- Lee family visits.

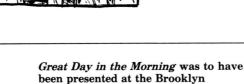

Great Day in the Morning was to have
been presented at the Brooklyn
Academy of Music this winter but a few
months ago performances were
postponed. Was *Great Day* withdrawn
so you could do some more work on it,
as some have suggested, or was it once
again a matter of financing?

Financing and time. There wasn't
enough time to mount it properly.
The work is in a finished state though
I do intend to make a few changes. It
will be performed in the future,
possibly at Covent Garden and La
Scala. It may also go to Africa and
Moscow.

**During the past year you also produced
The Golden Windows at the Munich
Kammerspiele, a new work featuring
one of your own texts.**

Yes. My text. I also designed,
directed and lit it. It's a smaller-scale
work. I built a little house.

It's early evening. There's a door that
opens—light streams from the
doorway. Then midnight.

The house is in the center. Then the
early morning.

The house is now at the left side of
the stage. Those three perspectives.

**The title of the work and perhaps a few
of its images were suggested by a story
in a now forgotten book of homiletic
fables by the American writer Laura E.
Richards (1903). What was the attraction
of this obscure story book?**

It was a fairy tale I heard as a child.
I just remembered the story. Actually

III,D

Knee Play 8:
- 19th Century Japanese basket
  sellers: Basket Dance.
- One basket falls from the stack
  and a small boy climbs out.
- He attaches the basket to a hot
  air balloon.

- Boy sails off in balloon.
- Balloon drifts to Africa;
  passes man in tree with lion
  beneath.
- Elephant,giraffe,zebra,tiger.

-Boy and balloon drift to Cyprus.
-A castle with two knights fighting;
  dead people on ground.
-Richard the Lionhearted enters
  with bride,from castle.
-Drunken guests emerge. Orgy.

-Balloon drifts to moon;Orange and
  Green landscape.
-The boy walks across the moon.
-Moon animals scurry by.

-Balloon drifts to Grand Canyon
  and descends.
-Indians fight.

-At bottom of Canyon,the boy enters
  with four others in an Oldsmobile.
-Mechanical gestures.

-The party from the Oldsmobile
  picnic and then leave.
-Boy remains behind,lying on the
  ground and laughing.

III,E

Knee Play 9:
- The cabin floats ashore.
- Cabin opens up to reveal a
  minstrel show as Japanese
  people watch.

- Rows of tents;preparation for
  battle.
- Sound of terrified animals.
- Oldsmobile enters with two people,
  singing.

- Soldiers slowly awaken and con-
  verse.
- Oldsmobile with people sing and
  speak.

- Soldiers gather and move off.
- Oldsmobile with people singing
  remains.

END OF ACT III.

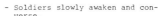
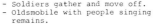

I had written the play before I thought of the title. The title didn't have anything to do with the play necessarily, but then it became part of it.

In the story a little boy gazes at a house on a distant hill which seems to have windows of gold and diamonds. One day he travels to the neighboring hill only to find a common farmhouse with ordinary glass windows. At the end of the story another house with golden windows appears to him in the distance. It is his own house, transfigured by the light of the setting sun. While *The Golden Windows* isn't based on this story, or even directly related to it, the two works do share the image of a house on a hill—a house whose appearance changes according to the

time of day it is viewed—and most importantly, a sense of the transforming power of light.

Light plays an integral role in the work. It's like an actor. Mainly, though, I just liked the title.

The play was performed in German and you worked with actors of the Kammerspiele.

Yes. I used members of their repertory company. Brilliant, brilliant actors. I think it's the most difficult thing for actors of the Schaubühne or the Kammerspiele to perform my texts because they don't tell a story. That's what all their training is aimed at—telling a story, interpreting a text, psychological theater. And if you do that with my works the

audience gets confused. You have to be able to say the text in a way that one can think about many sorts of things. If you say it in such a way that you must pay attention to every word you'll go crazy because one thought doesn't follow another thought logically. One thought can set off many thoughts. You have to sort of float with the situation.

Do you think this work will ever be seen in America?

There's a possibility that *The Golden Windows* could come to the United States in the summer or autumn of 1985. That will be the first time I have any time to stage it because I'm scheduled to do other things.

ACT IV is a film,compiled from various film archives, comprised
of sequences of natural disasters and times of conflict. On a
platform in front of the screen, a play is enacted depicting
the family unit in stories of struggle and survival throughout
history.

Knee Play 10:
- Night,snow,a Civil War tent.
- Three people pull boat hull
  from the water.
- A fourth person enters with a lan-
  tern and sees writing on the hull.
- They all read the writing.

(Some ideas to be included in the
compilation film)

- 100 Children playing in a field.
- King Harold.

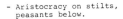
- Aristocracy on stilts,
  peasants below.

France,1815
- Napoleon enters on horse
  with troops.
- Louis XVIII with people in palace
  packing.

USA:Chatanooga
- Men climbing up rocks with ladders,
  firing into empty space.
- Union wins.

- Large Rock,center.
- Indians fighting,maybe a war dance.

Japan,March 24,1185.
- Battle of Dan no Ura.
- Baby emperor thrown over.
- Cherry blossoms fall into water.

IV (cont.)

Japan,February,1877.
- Snow.
- Samurais, Imperial Army.
- A tall Samurai,"Saigo".

-Animals
-League of Princes.
-Henry IV.

Spain,1936:
-Ruined University of Madrid.
-Condor Legion.

Dresden,1756:
- Frederick the Great approaches.

- Taking of Osaka.
- Ninjas jumping.

- Aristocrats.
- Civilian peace march.

-World War I.

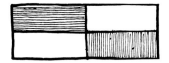

American audiences have not seen a major Wilson work since *Einstein on the Beach* was presented here in 1976. Money is invariably given as the reason so few of your productions reach this country. Is it solely a matter of financing or are other factors involved?

Financing has a lot to do with it. The other problem is where do you put it. Where do you put a work like *The Golden Windows*? In Munich I'm at the Kammerspiele, a municipal theater where I'm seen by a subscription audience. I have a poster from the Kammerspiele. Look at their season—they have plays by Chekhov, Shakespeare, they have *Medea*, a Sean O'Casey play, Goethe's *Tasso* and they have my work. Where in this city would you find a program like that?

The resident theaters in this country might conceivably be a place where your work could be seen. Have you approached them?

They haven't approached me, you can put it that way. Yes, I have gone to them on occasion but I don't have time to now. I have too many other things to do.

What about the Metropolitan Opera? There was discussion at one point about an operatic version of *Death Destruction and Detroit*.

Well, we had talked about it. I guess I'm not a popular person at the Met.

You've also reached a stage in your career where you no longer have to accept compromise. You're in demand at

IV (cont.)

All Countries:
- Kaleidoscope:people,objects, etc. fill entire frame of proscenium.

- Continue

-Continue

-Continue

-Continue

Epilogue;

- An owl on a tree branch.
- A tall Lincoln slowly crosses the stage.
- Earth Mother figure
- Trio is sung.

END OF ACT IV.

V,A

Knee Play 11:

- Tropical Jungle almost conceals hull.
- Three people discover the hull and begin to strip bark from it to assemble a book.

Dance.

- Cutout drops of suspension-bridge cables in outer space.

Dance.

Dance.

Dance.

---

subsidized European state theaters and festivals, organizations far better equipped to meet your exacting standards. Theater in this country usually means compromising in terms of just getting a play on.**

Entirely true. The Met is a very well-organized house and the labor is probably the best in the world for working with time. Still, they don't light a show the way I do. They don't rehearse the way I rehearse. There's not the same attention placed on detail. Lighting is an important part of my work. I usually spend years on my drawings and days setting light cues. Over here they light a show in eight hours. It's very hard to do the kind of work I do in structures in this country, it really needs a festival structure. And again there's the cost. *the CIVIL warS* in Los Angeles will be two and a half million dollars for three performances and that doesn't even include artists' fees. It's insane. Budgets, unions. *Einstein on the Beach* at the Metropolitan Opera cost $90,000 per performance. Just to run a show that was already created.

The technical demands of your works also present certain difficulties. A Robert Wilson play can no longer be staged just anywhere.

My work is unique, it means big houses. I work best in a large scale.

You don't plan to produce your own shows in this country as you sometimes did in the past?

I can't, though really in some way I do. Contracts with houses and unions. It's a whole profession. As a producer I'm not knowledgeable.

In the past you've spoken with some bitterness of this country's lack of support for your work. Now that you're so busy creating works for the leading theaters and opera houses of Europe is this still such a concern with you?

It's . . . a frustration. I don't want to be an expatriate but that's the way it is—I'm leaving this January and I don't come back until the very end of 1984.

In a recent interview you announced your intention to do more interpretive work in the coming years. *Great Day in

```
V,B                                              V,C
```

```
                                                 Knee Play 13:
Knee Play 12:
                                                 - The bush continues to grow
A library with a ladder.                           into a tree.
- A man enters and takes down a book.
- He goes to a desk and sits down and
  reads.
- The book turns green and a bush
  begins to grow from its pages.
```

```
Forest of birch trees.                           - The forest continues across
- Trees move slowly across stage.                  the stage, becoming denser and
- Chorus of animal sounds.                         more tropical.
- Robert E. Lee is seen through                  - Mrs Lincoln is seen as a child
  the window of a spaceship.                       trough the spaceship window.
```
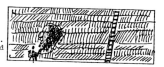

```
- Forest changes; autumn.                        - Chorus of Animals.
- Leaves fall off trees and green
  leaves grow in their place.
- A charred tree moves across.
- A singer and a chorus follow,
  singing Negro spirituals.
```

```
- Charred tree goes off.                         - Hercules, in a lion costume,
- Singers leave.                                   walks through the forest.
```

```
- A formal garden and trees                      - Hercules disappears.
  appear.                                        - Animal chorus,and voice of
                                                   Mrs. Lincoln.
```

```
                                                 Knee Play 14:

                                                 - The tree remains on stage.
                                                   In its upper branches a book
                                                   can be seen.
```

```
                                                 END OF ACT V.
```

the Morning, the first piece you've created to existing texts, represents a step in that direction. What was behind this decision?

The creation of new works is what I do best but I also think it's important to do other things, and so I want to interpret other people's work. I'm doing a new opera with Gavin Bryars, an English composer, which is based on Euripides' *Medea*. It will be performed at the opera house in Lyon and then will come to the Paris Opera.

What attracted you to this classic text?

I don't know. I just read the play and was fascinated by it. I liked the architecture of the story. It was very different from my work and yet similar in some ways.

Your *Medea* began life as a play with music. It's now a full-scale opera. What was the reason for this transformation?

I'd just rather hear words sung than spoken, I think. I'll also be doing another version of *Medea* in Lyon, a baroque opera by Charpentier which has never been performed. Then I'm doing *Four Saints in Three Acts*, the Gertrude Stein–Virgil Thomson opera, in Stuttgart in May of 1985. I also plan to do *Parsifal* in 1986 or 87, then a *King Lear*, yes, to Shakespeare's text, and maybe later I'll do some contemporary works.

KNEE PLAYS

Knee Play 1 (I,A):
-Man in a tree
-Lion beneath tree
-Silent
-Man in tree is hanging
-Goethe on a table
-Flying Vultures

Knee Play 2 (I,B):
-Two men have cut down tree
-Tree falls slowly
-Men carry tree off,and return with
 a log
-With another person, they attach
 log to a cabin

Knee Play 3 (I,C):
-Two men build a boat hull

Knee Play 4 (II,A):
-Three people finish building boat;
 they push it into water
-Another person enters with drink
 and they christen the boat.
-They sail off in boat.

Knee Play 5 (II,B):
-Boat sails on from SR
-Three people in boat
-A large bird flies down and carries
 one off as others watch

Knee Play 6 (II,C)
-Boat is beached on a rock
-Two people load the boat,then write
 on its hull

Knee Play 7 (III,A):
-Boat sails along a coast
-On Shore,two people load a cannon
 and fire at boat
-Boat is hit and breaks up;hull sinks
 but cabin floats on.

KNEE PLAYS (cont)

Knee Play 8 (III,D):
-19th Century Japanese basket-sellers:
 Basket-Dance.
-One basket falls from stack,and a
 small boy climbs out.
-He attaches basket to a hot air
 balloon.

Knee Play 9 (III,E):
-The cabin floats ashore
-Cabin opens up to reveal a minstrel
 show,as Japanese people watch.

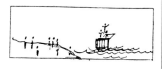

Knee Play 10 (IV,A):
-Night,Snow,a Civil War tent
-Three people pull boat hull from water
-A fourth person enters with a
 lantern and sees writing on the hull
-They all read the hull

Knee Play 11 (V,A):
-Tropical jungle almost conceals hull
-Three people discover the hull and
 begin to strip bark from it to
 assemble a book

Knee Play 12 (V,B):
A library with a ladder
-A man enters and takes down a book
-He goes to a desk and sits down and
 reads
-The book turns green and a bush
 begins to grow from its pages.

Knee Play 13 (V,C):
-The bush continues to grow into
 a tree.

Knee Play 14 (after V,C):
-The tree remains on stage.
- In its upper branches a book can be
 seen.

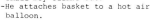

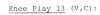

From time to time your work is described as a modern equivalent of Wagner's *Gesamtkunstwerk.* Now you are planning to produce several of the Wagnerian music dramas. I would be interested in knowing when you first encountered Wagner's music and at what point you contemplated staging his operas?

The Wagner family came to Spoleto when I did *A Letter for Queen Victoria* in 1974 and they said, "Oh, Mr. Wilson, it's so beautiful. You're the perfect one to do Wagner." Well, at that time I barely knew who Wagner was. So I said, "Thank you very much. I'm flattered." They asked me if I would be interested in coming to Bayreuth to direct something and I answered, "Well, possibly, but do you ever do new works because I'm really interested in creating *new* works." Gian-Carlo Menotti was sitting next to me and he started kicking me under the table. "No, no, we don't do new operas, Mr. Wilson. We only do Wagner." "Well," I said, "I'm really not interested just now." Then they asked me a couple of years later and I actually went to the festival. Finally they came when I did *Edison*—Wolfgang Wagner and his wife—and they said, "We're going to do a new *Parsifal* and we want to talk to you about that," and I said I was very interested in doing it. They said, "Well, Mr. Levine has already been contracted to conduct it. Could you work with him?" And I said, "Yes."

After so many years as a German (even a family) institution, Bayreuth has begun seeking outside talent. There was a French team (Chéreau and Boulez) for the centennial *Ring*. This summer's cycle will be essentially an English production (Hall, Solti and designer William Dudley). And you and Levine would have logically constituted an American team.

But Levine refused to work with me and he had already been contracted. It's sad. It was the hundredth anniversary. I mean, I don't particularly like Levine though there are some things he does conduct quite well, still I agreed to work with him because the best place to do *Parsifal* is, of course, Bayreuth.

Three-dimensional models for **the CIVIL warS**; designed by Robert Wilson and Tom Kamm; models created by Tom Kamm; 1983

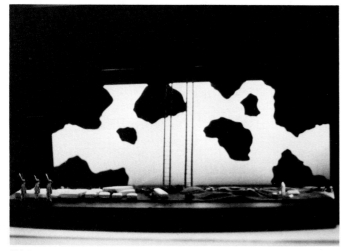

IA1

IB7

IA2

IB

IB3

IC2

IIB

IIC5

IIC4

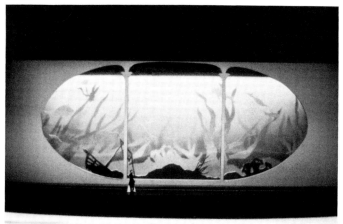

IIIA2

Later you were commissioned to create a *Parsifal* for the State Opera in Kassel, West Germany. Although this production was eventually canceled, I know you devoted a considerable amount of time to the project. I'd be interested in hearing how you set about approaching this monumental work, which would seem an ideal vehicle for you, resonating as it does so many of the themes and concerns of your own work.

Well, everyone always said *Parsifal* would be the work to do so I started to listen to the music and I hired Annette Michelson, a writer and scholar, to work with me for a number of months on a concept. I looked at various productions and found out what other people had done with the opera. There's a beautiful one that Appia designed and the one Wieland Wagner did in the fifties was really great, beautifully proportioned. I tried to find what Wagner was attempting to do musically and also what he was trying to say with the text. I'll only do one *Parsifal* in my life and I want this to be one of the great ones. So I thought about the

text and the music and the most complicated problem to solve was how to present a work that's very religious—it's very close to what I just did with Jessye—with a sincere religious attitude. It never seemed right to me to have this fake church service with these knights standing around singing and passing this holy grail. It was somehow sacrilegious, everything the work was supposed not to be. When I listen to the music here it's a religious experience but when I go to the theater and see this temple-church-whatever and these klutzy knights walking around with this cup, it's ridiculous, it's disturbing and it's all wrong. So that's one problem to solve. Then there's the idea that Parsifal is the innocent fool. How is that portrayed? Christopher Knowles would have been the perfect actor for me but someone like Manfred Jung playing this innocent fool is no good—it's no good in one sense, in another sense I guess it's O.K. You know when Levine does *Parsifal* at the Met there's a time in the third act when I feel I'm going to

IIIA5

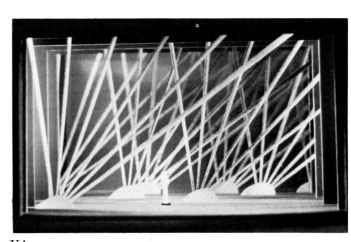

VA

IIIC2

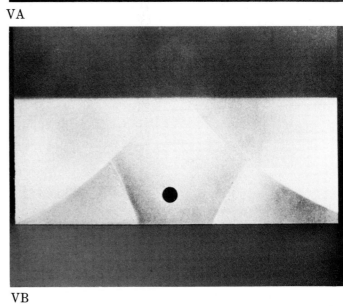

VB

IV Epilogue

VC

Hildegard Behrens and Robert Wilson in rehearsals for **the CIVIL warS**, Freiburg, 1983
▼

scream if he doesn't stop or he doesn't go faster. It's interminable. Yet it can be done in such a way that you say to yourself, "I can listen to this for the rest of my life." That's what's so fascinating about *Parsifal.* It can be unbearably long or it can be . . . forever. But the designs are all finished.

There's no house curtain. Instead there's a curtain of light.

Then a wall of water with the beams of light coming vertically across.

Eventually a lake appears at the back and that's the prelude.

The whole piece is in blue. Gurnemanz appears here at the downstage edge of the lake.

Just before Parsifal enters I have this enormous white swan, the swan that he's just shot, falling very slowly into the lake.

For the transformation scene—"Time becomes space here"—I have a great disk of light that moves on stage from the side and an iceberg floating upstage.

Eventually the disk of light settles in the center of the lake. Parsifal stands downstage watching with his back to the audience the way the audience watches it.

I don't have the knights or any of that. Amfortas is carried out in his litter and he goes into the iceberg and takes out an Egyptian box. Inside is a clear glass chalice which is shaped like an X.

He holds it up and then he disappears. At the end, Gurnemanz comes into the ring of light and asks Parsifal, "What have you seen?" And there's just the light, the whiteness. The idea is to make this mysterious temple of light. It's as if one were to see this big ring of light floating out here in the middle of the Hudson. It's all about light. And that's the first act. The second act starts the same way with the vertical beams of light crossing the water. We're still at the lake but now it's night and a metal tower rises out of the water.

It's like a fairy tale. That's where Chéreau missed the boat for me. His

114

Ring is beautiful looking, gorgeous, but it's so serious and heavy. And it's fantastic to have an opera with giants and a dragon, it's stories for children. Klingsor appears in a window in the tower and he's a bad guy almost the way Ivan the Terrible is in the movie. Kundry is next to him—and I want to do it with Jessye—and her hair falls out of the tower. After their scene, the doors close and the tower sinks beneath the waves. Then we go underwater for the flower garden scene.

There are ferns and painted flowers that open. They're all flat with lights inside them, only the rocks are dimensional. The flower garden is all in color. It's like Chinese flowers that open in the water. At the end of the act Klingsor throws his spear at Parsifal. Here it's a rod of light. The scene is all back painted and at the moment Parsifal picks up the glowing rod, we turn on all the lights from behind and everything appears in cold black and white like a skeleton. Parsifal takes the rod of light and draws the outline of the chalice in light, and that's the end of the second act. The third act begins the same way as the first except that I've put the singers on the other side of the stage. For springtime (the Good Friday scene), I've created an enormous tulip that's lowered into the lake, like the big swan you saw in the first act.

I also bring all the chorus onstage for one brief moment when they're trying to convince Amfortas to perform the grail ceremony. We have him lying in his litter and they rush on and form a huge wall of bodies downstage.

The ring of light comes back on. It's now a black disk, which slowly falls into the lake, turning white when Parsifal stands on it. He takes the chalice from the Egyptian box in the iceberg and holds it up. The iceberg disappears.

At the end he leaves the stage. No one is on stage. Fire comes out of the ring of light and stars appear in the sky.

In a sense what you've done is create your own mysteries within Wagner's larger ones. Your scenario also seems to have purged the opera of what many feel is its mock Christianity. What interests me even more is how you will approach the work's complex psychological characterizations. How will you deal with Wagner's characters and the acting requirements of the piece?

I can only tell you that it won't be psychological acting. It will be the opposite of what Chéreau did with the *Ring*. I never understood why they called that naturalistic acting. It's the most artificial, unnatural way of behaving on stage that I've ever seen in my life. But they all said that Chéreau has reinvented naturalistic acting. It's just too much for me. I'm not interested in that kind of thing.

While your *Parsifal* will be produced at some future date, it's regrettable you were denied the chance to stage the Bayreuth centennial production. The occasion demanded some kind of great event—either a radical re-evaluation of the work or a personal commentary by a major contemporary artist or at least a fresh sensibility. Certainly it provided an unparalleled opportunity in terms of visibility and critical attention. All things considered you probably would have been an ideal person for the job.

I would have been the ideal person, yeah.

Götz Frederich was eventually chosen to direct the centennial production, I believe at a relatively late date.

You know why? Because Frederich can come in and do it in two days. I saw a new production of *Tristan* he did two years ago in Stuttgart. It was the third *Tristan* he had done that year. I was there the night before the last general rehearsal and he still hadn't decided where the singers were going to be. It never *was* decided. In the second act he never even told them where to go. Now, how on this earth do you do that? They had one big vulgar spot that followed the singers wherever they went, and of course, they went where they normally go anyway. It's ridiculous. So that's why it went to Frederich. It's perfect for Levine and the way he thinks and the way they

run a house and the way they make art. And did you hear anything about the performances? No one even *mentioned* the *Parsifal* last summer. No one talked about it. The hundredth anniversary!

It's been rumored that you will be staging *Tristan* at Bayreuth some time in the future, possibly with Jessye Norman as Isolde.

Well, I would like to do it. I was asked. La Scala also asked me to do the *Parsifal* and I will if I get the rehearsal time I need. I would like Abbado to conduct, if he will work with me.

You're one of the few American directors who works regularly with a dramaturge, a fixture of the German state theater system. Was the concept of a dramaturge new to you when you went to Berlin in 1979 to stage *Death Destruction and Detroit* for the Schaubühne?

That's right. I always had various people around when I was working before—advisors, people who did research—but I never really had the concept of a dramaturge in mind. When they first gave me one in Berlin I said, "This is ridiculous." I walk in and there's a staff of twenty people. What are they all going to do? "A dramaturge?" I said, "I wrote the play! How is he going to tell me what I'm doing with this crazy American language and all?" But they were very, very helpful—I learned so much about what I was doing and about the possibilities of what could be done. I've since learned to work very closely with dramaturges and now I think it's almost essential to have one because I'm not scholarly, I don't have a strong background in history or a lot of formal or classical education and, anyway, it's very helpful to have someone like that to talk to. In Germany they've also translated my

texts so they have to be writers as
well as scholars because my texts are
difficult to translate—there's slang
and puns and things not immediately
translatable. At the Schaubühne I
worked with Peter Krumme, who was
excellent.

**Was he involved with the day-to-day
rehearsals?**

Yes, he was there all the time and
was directly involved with the actors
and their interpretations. We worked
as a team. When I produced *The
Golden Windows* in Munich, again a
fantasy thing with the kind of crazy
texts I do, I worked very closely with
Michael Wachsmann. He's brilliant
but he doesn't say very much.
"Maybe this word should be over
there" or "Take that out" or "Maybe
there should be a slight hesitation in

the middle of this word." I work with what they tell me, with what they feel is correct. It's very much a collaboration. I really like working with a dramaturge and I think they're underestimated—in terms of my work anyway.

While you've spent most of the last few years in Europe creating new works, you recently performed in Japan and will be returning there in the near future to produce several segments of *the CIVIL warS*. I'd think the Japanese would be an ideal audience, especially since the stylization, formality and durational qualities of their own theater forms logically prepare them for the imaginative demands of your work.

That's what everyone has said and I was very nervous about it. I did the prologue to the fourth act of *Deafman Glance*, which is a murder scene, with a beautiful Japanese actress (Chizuko Sugiura). It was actually one of the first things I ever made for the theater. They were a wonderful audience and it was very well received. There was a scholar who came and wrote a piece saying that the work was timeless but it happened in this century. In some ways the play is very modern but he saw that it was timeless, it could have happened any time. And that's the Japanese, they live with such an awareness of tradition and the past. They're very contemporary, very modern but they're still building houses with bamboo and paper.

You've made a number of video works in the last couple of years, some of which have been seen in this country. Are you planning to devote more time to media projects in the future?

I think TV is the future. To be very honest with you I don't watch it because it doesn't interest me, but at the same time I'm fascinated by the possibilities of the medium and am already planning more works with TV. I went to see Martha Graham's company when I was rehearsing an opera in Washington some time ago and I noticed that a work she had created in 1946 was listed in the program as having been copyrighted in 1977. I was told that she filmed it in 1977 and that established the

copyright. That's what I want to do with my works. People are asking about *Einstein* in particular, and I will do it again some place and film it.

Your works tend to play to a select, somewhat narrow audience made up of fans, theater people, writers, artists and art patrons. You've spoken in the past of wanting to attract new audiences to your work.

Right.

Are you still actively seeking a larger audience?

Absolutely. I think that's what I'm trying to do with *the CIVIL warS*. It's on the scale of large popular theater. That's how I intended it. It's an event, a large popular event. It's meant to be the way rock concerts are. I was in Rome a few weeks ago and Syberberg's film of *Parsifal*, which is four and a half hours long, was shown before three thousand people in a large open air space. It was fantastic. It was a big event. There was something exciting about being there, just like at a rock concert. I saw this *Napoleon* film at Radio City Music Hall and it was very exciting. It was in Japan when I was there. Everywhere it's been, it's been something special. It's an event and I think that's great. When I first went to hear a rock concert about fifteen years ago I thought, "Gee, this is really the great opera of our time." I don't think that when I go to the Metropolitan Opera. Maybe I do if I go to see Patrice Chéreau's *Lulu* at the Paris Opera. That's a great cultural event, but I don't go expecting such an experience at the Met. I mean, who's going to fly from Paris to see something at the Met? Chéreau just did *Peer Gynt* in Paris and people came from all over Europe. People went to Berlin for Peter Stein's *Oresteia*. That's an event. People come from all over Europe to see *The Golden Windows* in Munich. Who comes to Broadway to see *Sweeney Todd?* Who goes to see another John Dexter production at the Metropolitan Opera? Nobody! Nobody is interested. That's what's so *dull* about this city. No one comes

here to see anything. People come from New Jersey to see Broadway musicals. It's all for a suburban audience.

What about dance and avant-garde theater?

Well, if I want to see the avant-garde of America I'll go to Europe. You can't see it here. Richard Foreman is working at the Paris Opera. I just saw his new piece at the Festival of Autumn. I go to Europe to see that kind of thing, not America. Maybe people will go to the Village to see Joe Papp's work if there's something special about it but Joe presents his work for an audience that is very select, very narrow. He calls it a public theater, a popular theater, but I don't think it's that at all.

Do you think you can attract a popular audience as such to *the CIVIL warS?*

I hope so. I hope we get it done.

Entrance to **Poles** 1967. Grailville,
Loveland, Ohio

Poles 1967

Installation. Musée Galliera, Paris.
1974

Small Overture Chair. Musée
Galliera, Paris. 1974

Hanging Chair (Freud Chair) 1977.
Wire mesh. Collection: R.S.M.
Company

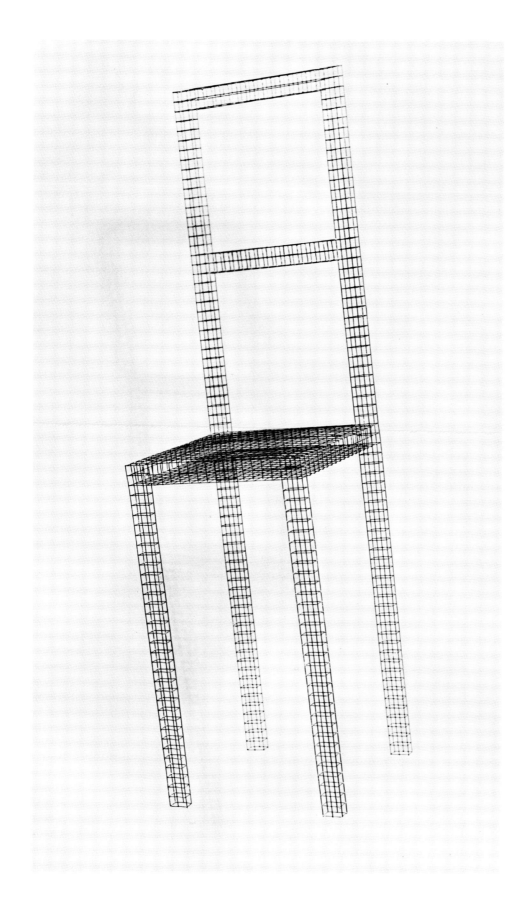

Flying Bench 1977. Wire mesh and
safety belt. Courtesy: Marian
Goodman Gallery

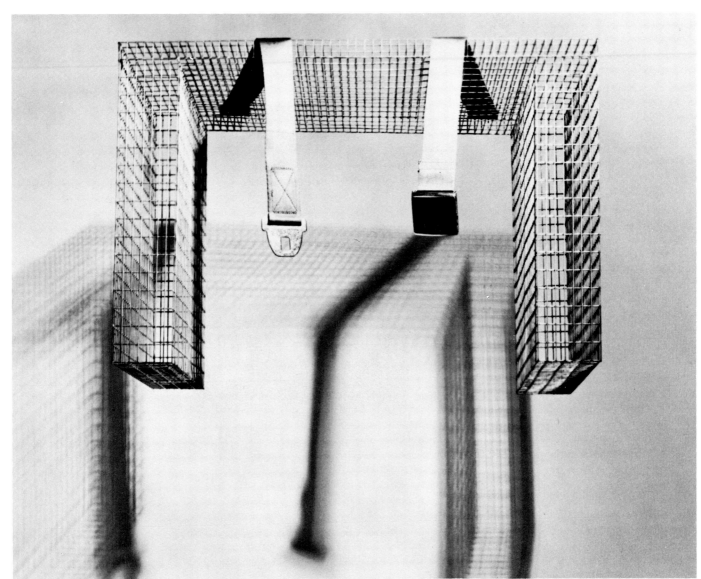

Overture Chair Oak, brass, vinyl,
water, acetylene gas. Installation:
Musée Galliera, Paris, 1974

Stalin Chairs 1977. Lead draped
over armature. Collection: Dr. Alvin
E. Friedman-Kien

Queen Victoria Chairs 1977. Lead,
brass, electric lights. Collection: M.
and Mme. Michel David-Weill

Einstein Chair, 1976. Galvanized
pipe. Collection: Paul F. Walter

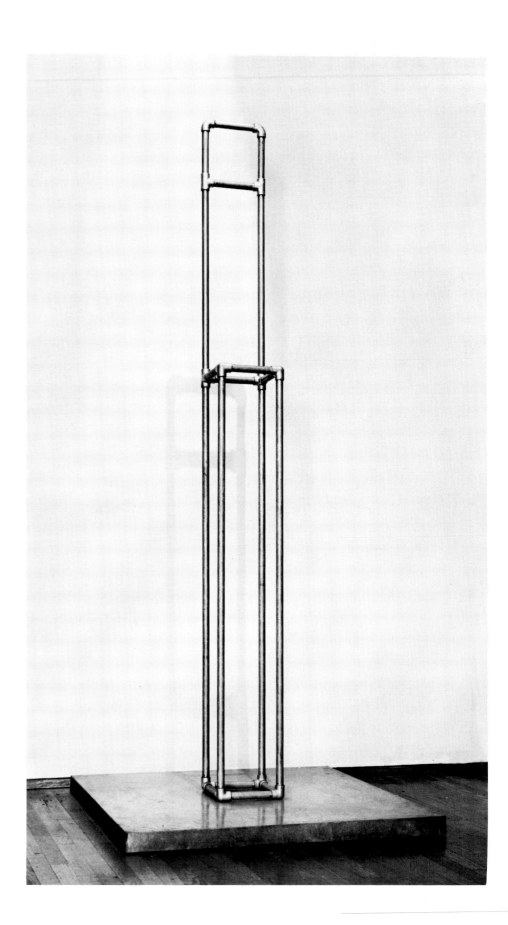

Patio Sofa 1977. Stainless steel.
Collection: Robert Wilson, Byrd
Hoffman Foundation

Light Bulb 1979. Glass, metal, neon.
Installation view with photostats.
Courtesy: Marian Goodman Gallery

Beach Chairs 1979. Aluminum.
Collection: Schaubühne am
Halleschen Ufer

Working drawings for **Spaceman**
1975. Felt pen and ballpoint pen on
paper. Collection: Paul F. Walter

Working drawing for **Einstein on
the Beach** 1976. Graphite on paper.
Collection: Paul F. Walter

Working drawing for **I Was Sitting
On My Patio This Guy Appeared I
Thought I Was Hallucinating**
1976. Ballpoint pen on paper.
Collection: Paul F. Walter

138

Suite of 13 drawings for **Einstein on the Beach** 1976. Graphite on paper.
Collection: William Kistler

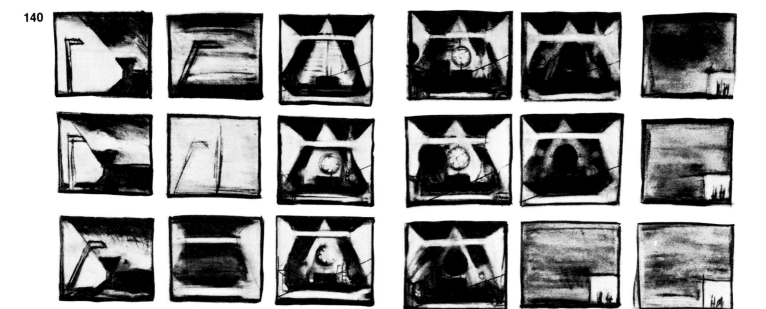

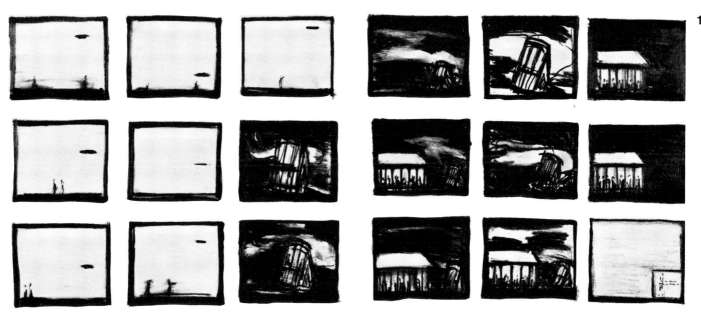

142

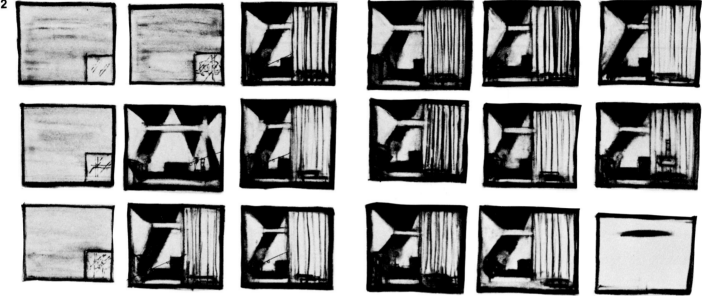

Knee Play, **Einstein on the Beach**
1976. Graphite on paper. Collection:
Taya Thurman

146

First Train Scene, **Einstein on the Beach** 1976. Graphite on paper. Collection: Mrs. Anna Walter

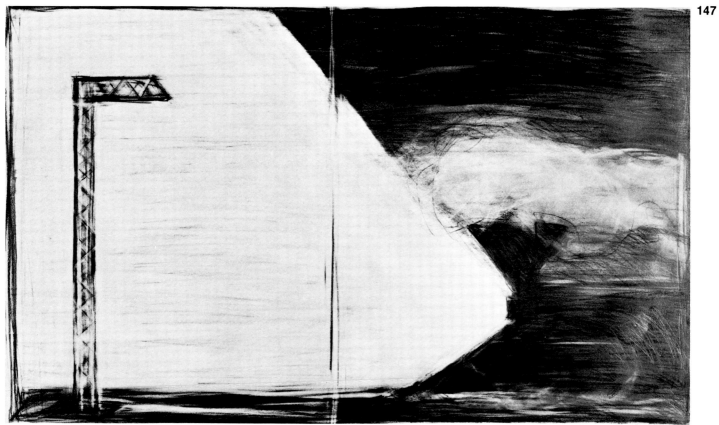

Building, **Einstein on the Beach**
1976. Graphite on paper. Collection:
Barbara Jakobson

Black Books and Sofa, **I Was Sitting On My Patio This Guy Appeared I Thought I Was Hallucinating**
1977. Graphite on paper. Courtesy:
Paula Cooper Gallery

White Arches, **I Was Sitting On My Patio This Guy Appeared I Thought I Was Hallucinating**
1977. Graphite on paper.
Collection: Toni Birckhead

Mountain, **Death Destruction and Detroit** 1977. Graphite on paper. Private collection.

Robert Wilson
Born: Waco, Texas, 1941

Education

1959-1965—University of Texas

1962—Studied painting with George McNeil, Paris, France

1965—Pratt Institute, Brooklyn, New York, B.F.A. Architecture

1966—Apprentice to Paolo Soleri, Arcosanti community, Arizona

Exhibitions and Related Activity

1963—Designed Jean Claude van Itallie's original production of "America Hurrah"

1963—Made two hour 16mm film, "The House", made film, "Slant", for WNET-TV

1967—Designed and built giant outdoor environment/theater/sculpture, "Poles", under commission for Grailville, Loveland, Ohio

1971—Made 16mm film,"Overture for a Deafman"

1971—Exhibition, Willard Gallery, New York

1972—Exhibited drawings and sculpture at Musée Galliera, Paris, France

1974—Drawings/Performance (with Christopher Knowles), Ala Gallery, Milan, Italy

1975—One-Man Show, Galerie Wunsche, Bonn, Germany

1975—Group Show, Paula Cooper Gallery, New York

1976—Video Performance, "Spaceman", The Kitchen, New York

1976—One Man Show, Iolas Gallery, New York

1977—One-Man Show, Galerie Skulima, West Berlin

1977—One Man Show, Multiples/ Marian Goodman Gallery, New York

1978—One Man Show, Paula Cooper Gallery, New York

1979—One Man Show, Galerie Zwirner, Cologne, Germany

1979—One Man Show, Multiples/ Marian Goodman Gallery, New York

Performances

Dance Event
1965—New York World's Fair, New York

Solo Performance
1966—Byrd Hoffman Studio, New York

Theater Activity
1967—Bleecker Street Cinema, New York

ByrdwoMAN
1968—Byrd Hoffman Studio, New York

The King of Spain
1969—Anderson Theater, New York

The Life and Times of Sigmund Freud
1969—Brooklyn Academy of Music Opera House, New York (two productions)

Deafman Glance
1970—University Theatre, Iowa City, Iowa

1971—Brooklyn Academy of Music Opera House, New York; Grand Théâtre de la Nancy, Nancy, France; Teatro Eliseo, Rome, Italy; Théâtre de la Musique, Paris, France; Stadsschouwburg Theater, Amsterdam

Program Prologue Now, Overture for a Deafman
1971—Espace Pierre Cardin, Paris, France

Overture
1972—Byrd Hoffman Studio, New York; Khaneh-e Zinatolmolk, Shiraz, Iran, Musée Galliera and Opéra-Comique, Paris, France

KA MOUNTAIN, GUARDenia TERRACE, a story about a family and some people changing
1972—Haft Tan Mountain, Shiraz, Iran

king lyre and lady in the wasteland, Part of "Solos"
1973—Byrd Hoffman Studio, New York

The Life and Times of Joseph Stalin
1973—Det Ny Theatre, Copenhagen, Denmark; Brooklyn Academy of Music Opera House, New York

DIA LOG/A MAD MAN A MAD GIANT A MAD DOG A MAD URGE A MAD FACE
1974—Teatro di Roma, Rome, Italy; John F. Kennedy Center, Washington, D.C.; on location Shiraz, Iran ·

The Life and Times of Dave Clark
1974—Teatro Municipal, São Paulo, Brazil

Prologue to A Letter for Queen Victoria
1974—Teatro 6 O'Clock Theatre, Spoleto, Italy

A Letter for Queen Victoria
1974—Teatro Caio Melisso, Spoleto, Italy; Municipal Theater, La Rochelle, France; BITEF Festival, Atelje 212, Belgrade, Yugoslavia; Theatre des Variétés, Paris, France; Theater II, Zurich, Switzerland; Maison des Arts et Loisirs, Thonon-les-Bains, France; Théâtre Municipal, Mulhouse, France; Maison des Arts et Loisirs, Sochaux-Doubs, France; Théâtre Huitième, Lyon, France; Palais de la Méditerranée, Nice, France; ANTA Theatre, New York

$ Value of Man
1975—Brooklyn Academy of Music Opera House, New York

To Street (solo performance)
1975—Bonn, Germany

DIA LOG with Christopher Knowles
1975—The Public Theatre, New York

DIA LOG with Lucinda Childs and Christopher Knowles
1976—Corcoran Gallery, Washington, D.C.; Whitney Museum, New York

Einstein on the Beach
1976—Festival d'Avignon; Deutsches Schauspielhaus, Hamburg, Germany; Festival d'Automne, Opéra-Comique, Paris, France; BITEF, Belgrade, Yugoslavia; Venice Biennale, Venice, Italy; La Monie, Brussels, Belgium; Rotterdamse Schouwburg, Rotterdam, Holland; Metropolitan Opera House, New York

I Was Sitting On My Patio This Guy Appeared I Thought I Was Hallucinating
1977—Quirk Auditorium, Eastern Michigan University; The Cherry Lane Theater, New York; Annenberg Center, Philadelphia; Fort Worth Art Museum, Fort Worth; Bayou Building Auditorium, University of Houston, Houston; Wilshire Ebel Theater, Los Angeles; Veterans Auditorium, San Francisco; Walker Art Center, Minneapolis

1978—Théâtre de la Renaissance, Paris; Rotterdamse Schouwburg, Rotterdam; Royal Theater, The Hague; Stadsschouwburg, Amsterdam; Theater II, Zurich; Théâtre de Carouge, Geneva; Piccolo Teatro, sponsored by La Scala, Milan; Theater Des Westens, Berlin; Staats Theater, Stuttgart; The Royal Court Theatre, London

Prologue to the 4th Act of Deafman Glance
1978—Manhattanville College, Purchase, New York; John Drew Theatre, Easthampton, New York

DIA LOG/NETWORK
1978—Institute of Contemporary Art, Boston, Massachusetts; Walker Art Center, Minneapolis; MoMing Collection, Chicago; John Drew Theatre, Easthampton, New York

Death Destruction and Detroit
1979—Schaubühne am Halleschen Ufer, Berlin, Germany

DIA LOG/Curious George
1979—Palais des Beaux Arts, sponsored by Kaaitheatre, Brussels, Belgium

154

Edison
1979—Lion Theatre (work in progress), New York; Théâtre National Populaire, Lyon, France (world première); Teatro Nationale, sponsored by La Scala, Milan, Italy; Théâtre de Paris, France

Prologue to 4th Act of Deafman Glance (solo performance)
1980—Raffinerie Plan K, Brussels, Belgium; Palais des Congrès, Liège, Belgium

DIA LOG/Curious George
1980—Teatro Nuovo, Torino, Italy; Festival of Ten Nations, Warsaw, Poland; Rotterdamse Schouwburg, Rotterdam, Holland

Medea
1981—Kennedy Center for the Performing Arts (work in progress), Washington, D.C.; Aaron Davis Hall, City College of New York

THE MAN IN THE RAINCOAT
1981—Theater der Welt, Cologne, West Germany

GREAT DAY IN THE MORNING
1982—Théâtre des Champs-Elysées, Paris, France

THE GOLDEN WINDOWS
1982—Munich Kammerspiele, Munich, West Germany

the CIVIL warS
1983—Schouwburg, Rotterdam, Holland; Théâtre de la Ville, Paris, France; Théâtre Municipal/Opéra, Nîmes, France; Maison de la Culture, Grenoble, France; Théâtre National Populaire, Lyon, France; Nouveau Théâtre de Nice, Nice, France; Salle du Conservatoire, Bordeaux, France; Grand Théâtre, Lille, France; Maison de la Culture, Le Havre, France; Schauspielhaus, Cologne, West Germany; Teatro dell'Opera, Rome, Italy; Walker Art Center, Minneapolis

Awards

1970—Best Foreign Play, 1970-71 (*Deafman Glance*), Le Syndicat de la critique et musicale, Paris, France

1971—Drama Desk Award for Direction (*Deafman Glance*), New York

1971—Sociétés des Auteurs et Compositeurs Dramatiques (Honorary Society), Member Adherent, Paris, France

1971—Guggenheim Foundation Fellowship Award, New York

1974—OBIE Special Award Citation for Direction (*The Life and Times of Joseph Stalin*), New York

1975—TONY nomination for Best Score and Lyrics (*A Letter for Queen Victoria*), New York

1975—Maharam Award for Best Set Design for a Broadway Show (*A Letter for Queen Victoria*), New York

1975—Rockefeller Foundation, playwriting fellowship

1977—Lumen Award for Design (*Einstein on the Beach*), New York

1977—Grand Prize (*Einstein on the Beach*), International Festival of Nations, Belgrade

1977—Critics Award for Best Musical Theater (*Einstein on the Beach*), Le Syndicat de la critique et musicale, Paris, France

1979—Top 10 Plays (*Death Destruction and Detroit*), German Critics Award, Berlin, West Germany

1979—First Prize (*Death Destruction and Detroit*), Germany Press for Playwright, Berlin, West Germany

1980—Guggenheim Foundation Fellowship Award, New York

Selected Bibliography

1970—"King of Spain" by Robert Wilson, *New American Plays* Vol. 3, William Hoffman, editor, Hill & Wang

1972—"The Byrd Hoffman School of Byrds", Nos. 81-82, *Cahiers*, Renaud Barrault

1973—*L'Art de Robert Wilson (Le Regard de Sourd)* by Stefan Brecht, trans. by Françoise Gallard in *Le Théâtre 1972.1*, ed. by Araball Christian Bourqois, Paris

1973—"Two Conversations with Edwin Denby; Publication for the Occasion of 'The Life and Times of Joseph Stalin' ", Byrd Hoffman Foundation, New York

1973—"Journey to Ka Mountain" by Basil Langton, *The Drama Review*

1973—"Ka Mountain and Guardenia Terrace" by Ossin Trilling, *The Drama Review*

1974—"A Letter for Queen Victoria" by Robert Wilson, calligraphy by Cynthia Lubar, Paris, France, Byrd Hoffman Foundation

1974—*Robert Wilson Dessins et Sculptures*, Musée Galliera

1975—"Time to Think—Profile on Robert Wilson" by Calvin Tomkins, *The New Yorker*, January 13. (Became a chapter in *The Scene* by Calvin Tomkins).

1975—"Dressing Robert Wilson's 'Life and Times of Joseph Stalin' ", *Theater Crafts*, May/June

1975—"The $ Value of Man" by Arnold Aronson, *The Drama Review*, September

1976—"Einstein on the Beach" by Robert Wilson and Philip Glass, EOS Enterprises, Inc., New York

1976—"Robert Wilson and Therapy" by Bill Simmer, *The Drama Review*, March

1976—"On Robert Wilson's 'Deafman Glance' " by Louis Aragon, *Performing Arts Journal*, Spring

1976—"Robert Wilson's 'Einstein on the Beach' " by Susan Flakes, *The Drama Review*, December

1976—"Il Teatro di Robert Wilson," by Franco Quadri, Venice Biennale, Venice, Italy.

1977—"The Theater of Images—A Letter for Queen Victoria" by Robert Wilson

1978—"I Was Sitting On My Patio This Guy Appeared I Thought I Was Hallucinating" by Robert Wilson, Byrd Hoffman Foundation, New York

1978—"I Was Sitting On My Patio This Guy Appeared I Thought I Was Hallucinating" by Robert Wilson, *Performing Arts Journal*, Volume IV, Numbers 1 and 2

1978—Gnome Baker II and III, Robert Wilson—From working notes for "Death Destruction and Detroit"

1979—"Death Destruction and Detroit" Schaubühne am Halleschen Ufer, Berlin

1979—"Einstein on the Beach" recording by Robert Wilson and Philip Glass, Tomato Records, New York

1979—"The Theatre of Visions: Robert Wilson," Stefan Brecht, Frankfurt, Germany, Suhrkamp Verlag

1979—" 'Death Destruction and Detroit—Robert Wilson's Tale of Two Cities,' " Performance Art, Vol. 1, No. 1, Pgs. 3-7.

Catalogue of the Exhibition

all dimensions in inches
height precedes width precedes depth

1
Hanging Chair (Freud Chair), 1977
The Life and Times of Sigmund Freud 1969
wire mesh
35½ x 9½ x 9½
Collection: R.S.M. Company, Cincinnati

2
Flying Bench, 1977
Deafman Glance 1971
wire mesh and safety belt
18 x 28 x 14½
Courtesy: Marian Goodman Gallery, New York

3
Overture Chair, 1980
Overture 1972
oak, brass, vinyl, water, acetylene gas
chair: 54 x 36 x 36, platform: 24 x 72 x 72
tank: 13 x 156 x 228
Courtesy: Marian Goodman Gallery, New York

4
Stalin Chairs, 1977
The Life and Times of Joseph Stalin 1973
lead draped over armature
2 chairs—each 33 x 61 x 61
Collection: Dr. Alvin E. Friedman-Kien, New York

5
Queen Victoria Chairs, 1977
A Letter for Queen Victoria 1974
2 chairs—68½ x 47½ x 47½
Collection: M. and Mme. Michel David-Weill, Paris

6
Einstein Chair, 1976
Einstein on the Beach 1976
galvanized pipe
93½ x 10 x 10
Collection: Paul F. Walter, New York

7
Light Table, 1977
I Was Sitting On My Patio This Guy Appeared I Thought I Was Hallucinating 1977
stainless steel, plexiglass, electric light
29 x 48½ x 15
Collection: Robert Wilson, Byrd Hoffman Foundation, New York

8
Telephone Table, 1977
I Was Sitting On My Patio This Guy Appeared I Thought I Was Hallucinating 1977
stainless steel
9 x 12½ x 12
Collection: Robert Wilson, Byrd Hoffman Foundation, New York

9
Patio Sofa, 1977
I Was Sitting On My Patio This Guy Appeared I Thought I Was Hallucinating 1977
stainless steel
32½ x 65½ x 18½
Collection: Robert Wilson, Byrd Hoffman Foundation, New York

10
Beach Chairs, 1979
Death Destruction and Detroit 1979
aluminum
31 x 78⅝ x 23¾ and 22 x 78⅝ x 23¾
Collection: Schaubühne am Halleschen Ufer, Berlin, Germany

11
Light Bulb, 1979
Death Destruction and Detroit 1979
glass, metal, neon
34 x 17 x 17
Courtesy: Marian Goodman Gallery, New York

12
Dam Drop, 1974
A Letter for Queen Victoria 1974
and solo performances
paint on canvas, fluorescent light
180 x 300
Collection:Robert Wilson, Byrd Hoffman Foundation, New York

13
Scroll Drawing, 1974
A Letter for Queen Victoria 1974
graphite on paper
8½ x 286
Collection: Paul F. Walter, New York

14
Small Scroll Drawings, 1974
A Letter for Queen Victoria 1974
ink on paper
4 pieces variable lengths
Collection: Robert Wilson, Byrd Hoffman Foundation, New York

15
Scroll Drawing, 1976
Einstein on the Beach 1976
graphite on paper
36 x 181
Collection: Gilman Paper Company,
New York

16
Knee Play, 1976
Einstein on the Beach 1976
graphite on paper
22 x 29½
Collection: Taya Thurman, New York

17
First Train, 1976
Einstein on the Beach 1976
graphite on paper
29¾ x 40¹/₁₆
Collection: Mrs. Anna Walter

18
Building, 1976
Einstein on the Beach 1976
graphite on paper
30¾ x 41½
Collection: Barbara Jakobson, New
York

19
Suite of 13 Drawings, 1976
Einstein on the Beach 1976
graphite on paper
each of 13 — 9 x 10
Collection: William Kistler, New York

20
Trial, 1976
Einstein on the Beach 1976
graphite on paper
25⅞ x 40
Collection: William Kistler, New York

21
Trial/Jail, 1976
Einstein on the Beach 1976
graphite on paper
22 x 29¾
Collection: Kathleen Norris and
Patrick L. Veitch, New York

22
Spaceship, 1976
Einstein on the Beach 1976
graphite on paper
29½ x 41½
Collection: Paul F. Walter, New York

23
White Arches, 1977
**I Was Sitting On My Patio This
Guy Appeared I Thought I Was
Hallucinating** 1977
graphite on paper
21⅝ x 29½
Collection: Toni Birckhead,
Cincinnati

24
Black Books and Sofa, 1977
**I Was Sitting On My Patio This
Guy Appeared I Thought I Was
Hallucinating** 1977
graphite on paper
21¾ x 29¼
Courtesy, Paula Cooper Gallery, New
York

25
6 Drawings, 1977
**I Was Sitting On My Patio This
Guy Appeared I Thought I Was
Hallucinating** 1977
graphite on paper
various dimensions
Collection: Richard L. Feigen, New
York

26
16 Drawings, 1978
Death Destruction and Detroit
1979
graphite on paper
various dimensions
Collection: Richard L. Feigen, New
York

27
Mountain, 1978
Death Destruction and Detroit
1979
graphite on paper
20¾ x 27¾
Private Collection, New York

28-36
Small Sketches for various works,
1976-80
graphite and ink on paper
various dimensions
Collection: Paul F. Walter, New York

37
Drawing for Stage Drop,
Scene 2, 1978
Death Destruction and Detroit
1979
graphite on paper, photograph,
beveled glass
12¼ x 16
Courtesy: Multiples Gallery, New
York

38
Drawing for Stage Drop,
Scene 3, 1978
Death Destruction and Detroit
1979
graphite on paper, photograph,
beveled glass
12¼ x 16
Courtesy: Multiples Gallery, New
York

39
Drawings for Video-13, 1977
Video-13 (work in progress)
graphite on paper
5 sheets, overall dimensions:
36¼ x 388½
Collection: Robert Wilson, Byrd
Hoffman Foundation, New York

40
Video-50 1978-80
Version by ZDF, Mainz, Germany
Producer Delegate: Film Video
Collectif, Paris and Lausanne,
Switzerland
color, sound, 51 min.

41
Once Upon a Telephone Pole
1967
by Maclovia Rodriquez
16 mm film
sound, color, 10 min.

Photo Credits

Agence de Press Bernand, pages 75, 76
Catherine Allport 43
Maria Austria 16
Michel Biannoulatos, *L'Express* 38
Martin Bough 11, 12, 13 (bottom), 14, 19
Jean Clareboudt 25 (bottom)
Bahman Djalali 20, 21, 22
Enquerand 74, 79
Ivan Farkas 15, 17
Ron Forth 35 (top), 49 (top), 73 (top), 131, 132, 135-148, 151
courtesy Marian Goodman Gallery 13 (top), 18 (top), 25 (top), 55 (top), 127, 129, 130, 133, 134
Philippe Gras 24 (top and bottom), 26, 27
Lois Greenfield 40
Béatrice Heyligers 33, 35 (bottom)
Horst 58
Torben Huss 29
Jacqueline Hyde 89
eeva-inkeri 149, 150
Silas Jackson 94, 95, 97
Katherine Landman 45
Babette Mangolte 46, 47, 49 (bottom), 51, 52
Silvia Lelli Masotti 78
Jennifer Merin 30, 31
George Meron 116, 118
R. Nusimovici 24 (middle)
Carl Paler 28
Alan Mark Poul 113
Pietro Privitera 41
Dominick Pronzo 36, 42
Fulvio Roiter 48, 50
Oda Sternberg 91
K. Rusch 111
Mary Swift 89
Nathaniel Tilestone 55, 56, 57
Leo Van Velzen 62, 63, 92, 115, 117, 118
Ruth Walz, frontispiece, 65, 66, 69-73
Gert Weigelt 86, 87
photographer unknown 18, 34, 58

All other photographs courtesy The Byrd Hoffman Foundation